9249* by Mary Haylock

"Thin, I think,
that fabric between realities.
Maybe minds aren't lost.
Maybe they just slip through
and find a different place to wander."

— C.J. Tudor, *(The Chalk Man)*

9249 by Mary Haylock*

9249*

by

Mary Haylock

720 – Sixth Street, Box # 5
New Westminster, BC
V3C 3C5   CANADA

9249* by Mary Haylock

Title: 9249*
Author: Mary Haylock
Publisher: Silver Bow Publishing
ISBN: 9782774030486
Cover Art: "Seeing Through" by Candice James
Editor: Sharla Cuthbertson

All rights reserved including the right to reproduce or translate this book or any portions thereof, in any form without the permission of the publisher. Except for the use of short passages for review purposes, no part of this book may be reproduced, in part or in whole, or transmitted in any form or by any means, electronically or mechanically, including photocopying, recording, or any information or storage retrieval system without prior permission in writing from the publisher or a licence from the Canadian Copyright Collective Agency (Access Copyright).

www.silverbowpublishing.com
info@silverbowpublishing.com

ISBN: 9781774030486 Print Book
ISBN: 9781774030493 E-Book

Library and Archives Canada Cataloguing in Publication

Title: 9249* / by Mary Haylock.
Other titles: Nine thousand two hundred forty-nine | Nine two four nine
Names: Haylock, Mary, 1939- author.
Identifiers: Canadiana (print) 20190120428 | Canadiana (ebook) 20190120479 | ISBN 9781774030486
  (softcover) | ISBN 9781774030493 (HTML)
Classification: LCC PS8615.A845 A692 2019 | DDC C813/.6—dc23

9249* by Mary Haylock

For my friend Lou,
with love

9249 by Mary Haylock*

FOREWORD

There is nothing funny about Alzheimer's disease. How awful to think of such a thing. But when Amy Winston, age 75, decides to liberate her childhood friend Clara from the Daffodil ward of Spring Garden Manor, there are plenty of laughs. Amy has never been one to take no for an answer, so she devises a diabolical plot to spring her pal that involves, of all things, a whole lot of red licorice. A clever idea indeed, but is it clever enough to fool Mr. Randall, the youthful director of the facility? He's the one who guards the key to the ankle bracelet that holds Clara captive. When Amy's plan somehow miraculously succeeds, the two old friends take off for the south with hopeless expectations of a better life once Clara is freed from her medicated stupor.

In truth there is nothing funny about this horrible disease, but in the midst of the heartbreak, there is a message of hope and enduring love here, and sometimes you just have to laugh at the indomitable spirit of these two geriatric gypsies who are determined to go down fighting.

9249* by Mary Haylock

9249* by Mary Haylock

Chapter 1

Amy Winston knew the code by heart, 9... 2... 4... 9* She bent from the waist, peering through the bottom of her trifocals to see the worn numerals on the keypad guarding the entrance to the Daffodil ward of Spring Garden Manor, aka, 'Lockdown'. She punched in the correct sequence slowly, pausing after each selection to realign her glasses that kept slipping to the end of her nose. The small light above the keypad turned from red to green and Amy grabbed the handle quickly, pushing open the heavy metal door before it changed its mind. She slipped inside as the door pulled itself from her fingers and closed behind her. Clank. It was an ominous, forever kind of sound.

Amy straightened her back, tossed the end of her multi-coloured scarf over her shoulder and with a defiant lift of her chin set out on her quest through the long shining hallways lined with framed Tom Thompson prints to find her friend, Clara.

As she picked her way among the small tables in the dining area, Amy greeted a few of the residents who sat at their places, heads bowed in a somnambulant dream state as they waited for their lunch, still an hour away. One or two looked up as she passed by, but no one spoke in answer to her cheery hello. They seemed to focus on a distant spot to the left or right of her, never letting their eyes meet hers, afraid of what they might see.

Clara must be in her room. Amy left the dining room and turned down another long corridor of doors until she came to the last one on the left where a small plaque held a neatly printed card that read, "Clara Cunningham". By sliding a new card into the metal channels of the sign, it could easily be changed to another name when the time came. Easy come, easy go, thought Amy. The door was closed, as usual, and Amy tapped lightly before pushing it open. The curtain on the one big window in the room was drawn shut but Amy could see a small figure outlined beneath the blanket on the bed, just a bit of grey curly hair poking out the top.

"Clara. Wake up, honey. It's me."

The shape on the bed moaned and turned over slowly. Two milky blue eyes peered up over the edge of the blanket staring blankly at Amy. Then Clara frowned and something happened in her eyes, a barely discernable flicker of recognition. Amy felt that rush of relief that always filled her heart when she sensed that Clara knew her. Pulling the blanket away from Clara's face, Amy planted a kiss on her old friend's soft white cheek.

"Get up, lazybones," Amy ordered. "Let's blow this pop stand."

Slowly, Clara untangled herself from the confines of the blanket and sat up on the edge of the bed. She was fully dressed in a pair of well-worn jeans and a faded blue sweater that matched the colour of her eyes perfectly. Her shoes and socks were still in place and on top of the sock on her right ankle, the electronic bracelet that kept her captive was visible. The sight of it made Amy clench her teeth. How dare they shackle that small frail body as though Clara were some kind of dangerous criminal. At seventy-five it was doubtful that Clara could harm anyone now.

Things were different when they were young. Amy smiled to herself as she remembered Clara at sixteen, tossing her blue-black curls in the sunshine at the beach, fixing her gaze on some hapless male who had wandered into dangerous territory near the towel on which Clara had artfully arranged her tiny tanned body, luring him to his doom with that coquettish smile. She was a piece of work in those days. A far cry from the pathetic little figure who sat obediently looking at Amy, waiting to be told what to do next.

"Let's go out for lunch, Toots," Amy made her voice light and tried to sound ordinary, like this was something that happened every day, so as not to upset Clara. She knew that Clara didn't like change in her routine. It made her anxious. "Do you have to pee before we go?"

"No." Amy took her hands and pulled Clara up off the bed. She led her to the bathroom door, opened it and guided her toward the toilet. Clara turned around and sat down, jeans and all. Oh shit, it was going to be one of those days.

"Pull down your pants, silly." Clara obeyed instantly and sat down again, peering up at Amy with a hint of laughter in her eyes.

"Underpants too." Clara jumped up quickly and complied with the order, snapping off a salute to Amy as she sat down. A splashing sound began immediately and went on for quite a while.

"Good thing you didn't have to go," said Amy sarcastically. She handed Clara a wad of toilet paper. "Wipe your butt, Kiddo." Clara did as she was told and pulled up her pants as Amy turned on the water at the sink.

"Wash your hands. Now dry them and let's go. I'm getting hungry, aren't you?"

"No."

"Yes, you are. Where would you like to go?"

9249* by Mary Haylock

"Home," Clara replied without hesitation, staring intently at Amy who decided to ignore this remark.

"How about Swiss Chalet or Montana's?"

Clara's frown deepened. "I don't have any money."

"Don't worry, I hold the money. You know that. I always look after the money when we travel." Amy tossed this off casually to put Clara at ease. Sometimes it worked for a while. Not this time though.

"I won't be able to pay the bill." Clara sat down on the edge of the bed again and started to lie back against the pillow, closing her eyes.

"Oh no you don't," Amy protested. "Come on. It'll be all right."

"How will I pay? I don't have any money."

Amy looked down into the troubled face of her old friend. "I have your money. I always look after the money. Remember in Italy, who looked after the money?"

"You did?" Clara began to look more at ease.

"And Greece? And Portugal?" said Amy?

"Did we go there?"

"Yes. We went all those places and more, and I always looked after the money and it
was just fine. So, let's get out of here."

"I have to pee." Clara started toward the bathroom door.

12

9249* by Mary Haylock

"No, you don't. You just peed a minute ago. Let's go."

"Where are we going?"

"Out for lunch, if we ever get there."

"I don't have any money."

"Don't worry, it's my turn to pay. You paid last time, okay? Come on, let's go."

"Where?"

"Crazy!" It was a terrible thing to say. Amy was usually better able to keep her cool than this. After all, she used to teach five-year old children in kindergarten how to tie their shoes. Thirty of them. But that was a lifetime ago. I must be losing it, she thought. She took a deep breath and smiled reassuringly at Clara. Taking her hand, Amy guided her gently toward the door of the room. Clara stopped in the doorway.

"Where are we going?"

"Out for lunch."

"How will I pay?"

"Trust me."

Clara smiled sweetly up into Amy's face, slipped her arm through Amy's and snuggled into the familiar side of her friend.

Amy could feel wetness gathering under her arms as she marched down the hallway with Clara in tow. And this was only the first stage of the getting out process. When they reached the large dining room area, more of the residents had gathered at the tables, many of them dressed in large plaid bibs, heads bent over their placemats as if in prayer. Amy headed for the nurses' station. No one was there so she took Clara's coat and gloves from the closet where they were kept securely out of sight in case, she decided to go on one of her walks again.

That first walk several months ago had been Clara's biggest mistake. She had been in the Tulip ward back then. Many of the inmates there were more like her, walking about freely, watching tv, some of them even playing a game of cards or reading in a comfortable chair. There were no restraints to keep them there other than the locked front door. But on that lovely autumn day, Clara had probably looked through the large glass windows and noticed the trees with their golden leaves beckoning in the sunlight. She had slipped through the front door as a visitor came. No one knew she was gone until the front desk received a phone call from the police who had been summoned to a nearby home. Clara had gone there, and they had contacted the police who returned her to the Gardens. After that, Clara had been fitted with her ankle bracelet and moved to the Daffy ward, with its magic door. No matter how many combinations of numbers she tried, Clara could not make it work. And once when she slipped through again on the coat tails of some unsuspecting visitor, frightening alarms had gone off, driving her to hide behind a chair in the lounge until she was put back with the other Daffies. Eventually she gave up.

"Where are we going?" Clara sounded frightened as Amy guided her arms into the sleeves of her coat.

"Out for lunch, and yes, I know you don't have any money. The food is free today."

"I can't go outside." There was real fear in Clara's voice. "They won't let me."

9249* by Mary Haylock

"I'd like to see them stop us." Amy turned Clara around and zipped up her coat.

"Oh, they'll stop us." A worried frown creased Clara's forehead as she looked up into Amy's face.

"No, they won't. I'll run 'em through." Amy sounded fierce.

Clara giggled as they headed for the front door. "Snicker snack," she said, brandishing an imaginary sword in the air. Amy nodded to the volunteer manning the front desk who waved back and pushed a button to de-activate the alarm. Once more Amy bent to the task of pressing the buttons on the keypad. 1...2...3...4...* Easy to remember this time. She pushed open the door and pulled a reluctant Clara through to the foyer, then, holding tightly to Clara's hand, she signed the book to say what time they had gone out and when they would be back. With one push the front door swung open into the chilly air of the outside world and they were free. Clara stopped in the doorway.

"Where are we going?"

Amy took a big breath of the crisp, cold air. "We're going to Oz to get you a brain." She took Clara's hand and started to sing the title song from the Wizard of Oz.

Clara joined in as they both marched in time to the familiar tune. He'd have to be a Hell of a Wiz to fix you, Amy thought. As they tramped along the yellow brick road that led to the parking lot Amy marvelled at the way Clara could remember all the words to this and many other songs, when she couldn't remember who she was.

When they reached Amy's car, the singing stopped. Clara hesitated to get in.

9249* by Mary Haylock

"Where are we going?"

"Out to lunch, and God how I dread it."

Amy gave Clara a boost up into the passenger seat and reached across to do up the seat belt. Nose to nose they looked at each other for a moment. Then Clara grabbed the ends of Amy's scarf and pulled her closer, planting a kiss on Amy's startled lips.

"Let's blow this pop stand," Clara said.

9249* by Mary Haylock

Chapter 2

When she noticed Clara shivering in the seat beside her Amy turned up the heat in the car. It was always so hot in Spring Garden Manor that the residents became accustomed to living in the tropics. It was like taking a salamander out of its aquarium and sticking it in the freezer, Amy thought. Clara was busy singing. Now it was a familiar tune playing on the "Oldies" station that Amy liked to listen to on the car radio. Clara's tongue nimbly negotiated the tricky lyrics of *Anything Goes*.

Amy shook her head in wonder. What kind of a rolodex of musical numbers was lodged in Clara's poor gummed up brain and how did it manage to survive the ravages of the horrible disease that was slowly eating away at her mind? There was a lot to learn about Alzheimer's. Too late for Clara, probably, but hopefully in time for some of the other victims who were yet to come. Still Amy believed that some mental stimulation might help to stave off the inevitable and she was determined to provide as much as she could. Having lunch out at a restaurant didn't seem like much, but it would be a big deal for Clara. She'd have to rise to the occasion and use her wits, or what was left of them, to keep from embarrassing herself. Amy thought Clara was still capable of feeling upset when she did something stupid out in public. Somehow, she knew. The song ended and Clara resumed her worried expression.

"Where are we going?"

"Let's go to Montana's," Amy said. We can get a seat by the fire. That'll feel good on a cold day like this." The waitresses at Montana's knew them, so it wasn't quite so awkward when Clara did one of her unusual tricks, like suddenly standing up and waving at the other patrons or crawling under the table to hide when the food came. But she was pretty good today, Amy thought. Maybe this will be a good day. They pulled up in front of the restaurant and Clara looked fearfully at the front door.

"I don't have any money."

"I have your money right here in my purse. You gave it to me, remember? Come on Honey, I'm hungry."

Amy went to the passenger door and opened it, then she undid Clara's seatbelt. Reluctantly Clara allowed herself to be led into the restaurant, following Amy closely as a duckling shadowing its mother. The waitress took them to a booth in the corner by the fireplace. They sat facing each other and when Amy slipped off her coat and gloves, Clara followed her lead and did the same. Then she picked up the menu and started to study it. For a split second it seemed just the way they had done it for years on their travels.

Friends since high school, they had been cast together by fate when Clara's husband left her for his blonde secretary and Amy's mate died suddenly. On their own again after all those years they set off to see the world. And for a while they had a ball. Until Amy started to notice that more and more Clara hung back about making decisions or going off on her own to visit some little church in Santorini or to go out with some of their fellow travellers to an Italian pub late at night. Clara had always been a night owl and Amy started to nod off at ten o'clock, so they often split up to go their own ways if it suited them. But more and more Clara relied on Amy to remember the hotel room key and the tour guide's instructions about what time to put the bags in the hall and be ready to board the bus. Finally, on a cruise in the Caribbean, when

Amy left her at a bar to go to the washroom, Clara tearfully accused Amy of trying to lose her on purpose. Later in their stateroom, Clara confessed that she couldn't remember their room number and had no way of finding her way back there by herself. At this point, Amy had to admit what she had long suspected. Clara's memory was failing. When they arrived in Fort Lauderdale and disembarked at the terminal, Clara followed some other tall grey-haired woman out to board a bus to Miami while Amy was busy retrieving their luggage. Amy saw her just in time waving happily at the window as the bus was pulling out. It was their last big trip together.

"I can't pay for this." Clara closed her menu and started to put on her coat.

"Yes, you can. Look, here's your money. Right here in my purse. See?"

Amy removed the small change purse attached to her wallet and handed it to Clara, who opened it and saw the twenty-dollar bill Amy had planted there. She sighed with relief, snapped the purse shut and picked up the menu again. Amy hoped the trick would work long enough for them to order their lunch.

The waitress smiled at Clara; pencil poised over her order pad. "What'll you girls have today

"I'm not hungry." Clara smiled back and closed her menu.

The waitress raised her eyebrows and looked at Amy.

"We'll have the meatloaf dinner, please. Both of us. And tea. Just one bill. Thank you."

"Okay, then." The waitress replied.

9249* by Mary Haylock

Amy handed her menu to the girl, who reached for Clara's menu. Clara pulled it away from her and put it in her lap.

"Thank you." Amy said. The waitress walked away shaking her head.

"I can pay, you know." Clara sounded defiant.

Amy pointed to the purse and Clara snapped it open. She took out the twenty and placed it carefully on the table. Then she took one of the paper napkins from its holder and began to roll it into a long white log. Amy settled back in her place. Now Clara would have something to occupy her for a while and Amy could relax a bit. There were twelve little logs on the table, precisely rolled and arranged in a straight line when the lunch arrived. Clara took another serviette and tucked it under her chin, smoothing it down the front of her sweater. She looked up at Amy and put her hands in her lap, on top of the menu.

"Eat up. It's your favourite, meatloaf. It smells wonderful," Amy said.

"Did I order meatloaf?"

"Yes. You said, 'Oh, boy! Meatloaf! I really love meatloaf!" Amy found it sometimes convenient that Clara couldn't remember things. She leaned across the table and put some meatloaf on Clara's fork.

"There you go. Eat up while it's still hot."

Clara opened her mouth obediently and let Amy feed her three mouthfuls before she pressed her lips together tightly and turned her face away.

"I don't like meatloaf."

"Yes, you do. You always say that meatloaf is better than lobster! You used to cook meatloaf for Christmas dinner. You even had meatloaf for your wedding supper."

"Am I married?" Clara opened her mouth and took another bite on her own. While she chewed, Amy wondered what to say. How to explain that bastard who had four daughters with Clara and then abandoned her.

"Not anymore, you're not. That was a long time ago. Do you remember him?"

"No."

For a while Clara had that faraway look in her eyes that Amy dreaded. Then she seemed to snap out of it and smiled across the table at Amy.

"Are we lesbians?"

Amy was caught completely off guard. "No! Are you nuts?" Why on God's green earth would you say that?

"Because I love you."

Amy didn't know what to say. This was something new. She leaned across and started to flatten Clara's mashed potatoes with her fork. Then she used her knife to cut them into squares the way her own father had done for her so many years ago.

"Eat your potatoes," Amy said.

Clara dug her fork into one of the squares and lifted it carefully out of the grid pattern Amy had made.

"Tic, tac, toe," said Clara, as she removed three squares in a diagonal line, happily popping them into her mouth without chewing or swallowing. Amy had a bite of her own meatloaf before she noticed Clara's bulging cheeks.

"Stop!" Amy's warning came too late. Clara began to choke on the next mouthful of mashed potatoes, coughing and spewing food across the table. Neighbouring diners looked up from their plates and then looked away quickly. Amy grabbed a handful of napkins and began mopping up the mess, starting with Clara's chin as the waitress hurried back to the table and used a large cloth to finish the clean up. Amy's lunch, which she had hardly touched was now spattered with white blobs of potato.

"Do you want another plate?" the waitress asked

"No, thanks. Just bring the bill, please." Amy began to feel a bit queasy. She put on her own coat and then helped Clara into hers. "Come on, Toots. I think we're finished now. Let's go."

As Clara stood up Amy noticed a spreading puddle of wetness on the seat of the wooden bench. She took off her scarf and wiped it up.

I have to pee." Clara announced matter-of-factly to the room at large.

Back behind the wheel of the car with Clara safely seated beside her on the car rug, Amy could feel her heartbeat slowing down to a more normal rate. She buckled Clara in and turned on the ignition. The radio started up again, a Neil Diamond song, and Clara joined in with gusto. *I Am I Cried!* To Amy the words seemed heartbreakingly appropriate.

When they got back to the Manor, Amy signed them in and waved through the window to the volunteer at the front desk, the guardian of the alarm, who switched it off so Clara could enter through the big front door. 1...2...3...4* and they were back safe in Tulip Ward.

"Well, where have you two gals been?" The volunteer had a loud hearty voice.

"Out getting drunk," Clara volunteered, imitating the woman's strident tone perfectly.

"Oh my." The woman glanced at Amy, scowling. "We aren't supposed to drink alcohol when we're taking meds. You know the rules, Mrs. Winston. It could have a very bad effect on Mrs. Cunningham." She wagged a finger at Amy.

"We weren't drinking, Elsie. Don't worry. Although I could use a stiff one right now." Amy suddenly felt very tired.

Clara's voice rang out loud and clear in the quiet of the afternoon, some kind of bawdy drinking ditty.

"Shut up, Clara." Amy said. But Clara was in great voice today and continued to sing.

"Really, Mrs. Winston, we can't have our residents drinking. I'll have to speak to Mr. Randall about this. And I know that Mrs. Cunningham's daughters wouldn't like to think that their mother was coming home from an outing with you in this inebriated condition."

"She's not drunk. She's just nuts!" Amy grabbed Clara by the coat sleeve and headed for the door to Daffodil Ward. As she punched in the code, 9...2...4...9...*, she hung onto Clara, who was in fine voice.

9249* by Mary Haylock

When the door opened, Amy hustled Clara along the empty hallways as quickly as she could. Most of the residents were in their rooms, doors closed, probably taking their narcotic-induced naps. She hoped Clara's clamoring wouldn't wake them up.

At last they reached Clara's room and Amy pushed her in. Clara stopped singing.

She took off her coat and dropped it to the floor, then climbed up on her bed, closed her eyes and seemed to drift instantly off to sleep. Amy covered Clara with the blanket at the foot of the bed, closed the curtain and picked Clara's coat up off the floor.

"So long, Kid. I'll see you in a few days. Be good." Amy was almost out the door when she heard a small tired voice from the bed.

Thanks, Amy. I miss you."

9249* by Mary Haylock

Chapter 3

On the way home from Spring Garden Manor, Amy allowed herself the luxury of a few self-indulgent tears. Lunch with Clara hadn't turned out the way she'd hoped. And really, what good had it done for either of them? Amy felt that familiar wave of despair washing over her. It was just like the one that had almost drowned her after Gord died, when nothing mattered anymore and sometimes the effort to get out of bed was more than she could muster.

that was B.C.... before Clara. Clara, the little dynamo who appeared at her door with a coffee every day, talking about ordinary things, planning an outing here or there with old friends, dragging her to the mall, forcing Amy to keep on living. And somehow, after a few months, Amy began to look forward to the day, and to Clara's visits and phone calls. Soon they became like Thelma and Louise. Clara and Amy, off to see the world together, making the most of whatever time they had left.

But now, with so many wonderful places to go and so much more still to do, Clara had left her too. Not suddenly, like Doug, but slowly and imperceptibly. At first Amy had ignored the changes. She tried to convince herself they were just little spells of forgetfulness, the inevitable memory lapses of old age that all her friends laughingly complained of. Walking into a room with great purpose and standing there, wondering why. Or peering into the refrigerator, trying to bring to mind what had prompted the opening of that door in the first place. They were all the same. It happened to everyone over the age of seventy … didn't it?

But it happened too often to Clara. She burned several pots on the stove beyond recognition before her daughters pulled the fuses and made her use the microwave instead. And after she went to the corner grocery store one day and ended up in a gas station a hundred miles from home, the girls confiscated her car telling her it needed repairs. Even after several months, Clara didn't question why the car was taking so long to get fixed. She complained about it when Amy came to pick her up for bridge or a lunch date, but the rest of the time she seemed to forget about it.

When Clara's oldest daughter Debbie called, Amy kept her mouth shut.

"You're such a sweetheart for taking mom out Amy. Thanks so much. We really appreciate the help. By the way, how was Mom when you guys went shopping the other day?" This seemingly innocent question put Amy on full alert.

"Fine. She bought a cute sweater at the Bay. Pink. It looks good on her."

Amy didn't mention that Clara had lost so much weight they shopped in the junior department now. She was down to a size four. Maybe they hadn't noticed. Amy suspected that Clara forgot to eat most of the time.

"Did you eat today?" Amy would ask when she saw the papery skin stretched tightly over the bones in Clara's nose.

"Yes, of course I did." No hesitation.

"What did you have?" Amy hoped to catch her in an obvious lie.

9249* by Mary Haylock

"Cheese and crackers." It was Clara's stock answer.

"Last time I looked in your fridge, your cheese was green and hairy."

"I bought some new stuff yesterday." Amy knew this wasn't true. But she didn't tell Clara's girls.

A bout of flu kept Amy at home in bed for a week. When she recovered, Clara was gone. Her daughters had moved quickly when a nursing home became available. They didn't tell Amy until the deed was done. She will be safe now, they said as they packed up their mother's things and got ready to sell her house. By the time Amy had recovered from her initial shock at the swiftness of Clara's incarceration, Clara had already taken that first ill-fated walk and been shackled and confined to the inner sanctum of Spring Garden Manor, the Daffodil Ward.

When Amy first visited her there, she hardly recognized the Clara she used to know. Instead she was greeted by the sight of a zombie with empty eyes, even thinner than the last time she had seen her, unresponsive to Amy's hugs and tearful kisses. Clara was drugged to the nines. How else could they keep that restless spirit locked up and easy to handle. And of course, there was that ankle bracelet, just in case she could muster the monumental effort to escape from her palliative prison and make a break for it. Was this the end of the road for Clara? Her mother had lived to be ninety-nine. Clara could be stuck there for another twenty years, shrouded in bubble wrap, safe as a church and out of her mind.

Amy didn't go back for two weeks. She couldn't bear it. But when she did, she was pleasantly surprised. Clara looked a bit fatter and had lost the grey complexion she had been sporting lately. Her eyes seemed able to focus and Amy thought she detected some sort of recognition in their troubled depths. Even though Clara didn't speak, Amy knew that she felt a connection of some kind to the woman who stood before her claiming to be her friend.

"It's me, Clara. I'm your best friend, Amy. You know me. We've known each other for sixty years."

Clara's worried expression softened a bit in response to Amy's words. Amy took her arm and led her to the window. Outside the trees were bare and the November wind was playing among the deserted branches. Grey clouds heralded the coming of the first snow. Clara and Amy stood by the window together, hand in hand, breathing in the familiar presence of each other.

By Christmas time in Spring Garden Manor Clara could almost pass for normal, Amy thought, whatever that was. She had gained more weight and the regular meals had improved her complexion and the condition of her hair considerably. She spoke more frequently now and volunteered an opinion once in a while, although often slightly off the topic of conversation:

"What do you want for Christmas, Clara?" Amy asked.

"I want to go home."

"How about a pretty new sweater? I'm getting tired of that blue one you always wear."

"My Christmas tree is pink."

"I know. You love pink. You always had the most beautiful Christmas tree. Pink ornaments everywhere."

"The angel goes on top."

"It's a lovely angel. I remember her. So shiny."

9249* by Mary Haylock

"I can't find my diamond earrings. Debbie is mad at me."

"Where did you put them?"

Clara's struggle to remember was reflected in the frown on her face.

"Can I lie down now?"

"Sure." Amy left the present she had brought on Clara's nightstand. A new pink sweater. She never saw it again.

Clara's girls took her to Debbie's for Christmas dinner. Amy heard about it later. The whole family was there. Clara got up from the table, put her coat on and sat outside on the front steps in the snow while Debbie's husband was still carving the turkey. They took her back to the Manor before the pudding was served.

Poor girls. Amy sympathized with them. She knew what it was like to do something for Clara and then have it blow up in your face. Like this lunch today. Why did she bother? Clara missed a nice stew for lunch, and she'd be hungry by supper time. Why didn't she just give up and leave Clara alone? Was she really doing it to help Clara or was she doing it for herself, to make herself feel good? She liked it when people said, "That Amy. What a wonderful friend she is. She even takes her out for lunch. Clara is so lucky to have her."

Bullshit! All Clara wanted was to go home. Not to a restaurant or her daughter's house, but to her own place with the pink Christmas tree with the angel on top and the mouldy cheese in the fridge and her good jewellery carefully stashed away, somewhere they'd never find it, maybe in the bag of kitty litter in the basement where they found other precious things. If Amy was such a good friend, she'd take her away from the prison she was in. She'd take Clara home. Amy started to think about this. The more she thought about it, the more resolved she became to give Clara what she really wanted, that most precious of all gifts, freedom!

9249* by Mary Haylock

Chapter 4

"I miss you Amy." In the days that followed, Clara's last words kept running through Amy's head as she went about her affairs, shopping for groceries, taking her books back to the library, driving to the 'full serve' gas station for a fill up. Obviously, Clara had known who Amy was, remembered her name and still had feelings for her old friend. The unexpected kiss in the car was proof of that. She was not just an empty-headed shell who existed as some kind of slapstick ghost of her old self. The real Clara was in there behind those vacant eyes and Amy made up her mind to get her out. Out of her drugged state of docile compliance, out of her lethargic disengaged lifestyle and most of all out of her prison, the Daffy Ward of Spring Garden Manor. But how?

A plan began to take root in Amy's mind. She would take Clara away some place where no one would find them. Somewhere where she could bring Clara back to life again. Down south to Florida! She knew the way there like the back of her hand. I-90 out of Buffalo to 79 South. She and Gord had done it every year since he retired, spending most of the winter months in the sunshine state. That sunshine would be good for Clara, help her get rid of the prison pallor she had acquired from being indoors twenty-four seven. Amy smiled to herself remembering how Clara loved the beach. It wouldn't be easy, but Amy knew she could do it. And as an added bonus, she remembered she still had Clara's passport in her carry-on from their last trip. Her girls hadn't

31

thought about it or asked for it. They probably thought Clara had lost it, along with her jewellery.

They could rent a little place down the gulf coast, near the beach. Maybe in Fort Myers or Punta Gorda, where she and Gord used to go. Clara had visited them there for a few weeks every winter and she loved it. The three of them got along well and Gord loved to chauffeur them around in his old Lincoln town car. Driving Miss Lazy and Miss Crazy he would say. Amy knew her way around down there. She could do it too.

But first she had to get Clara out of Daffyland. That damned anklet that was attached to Clara had to be removed. How the hell did it work? Was there a key or did they weld it on somehow with a shiny metal alloy of some kind? Amy's great grandfather had been the blacksmith in the village where she grew up many years ago. She had seen pictures of him in her mother's house. A large, strong man with folded arms standing in front of his wooden blacksmith shop on the main drag. She called upon his spirit to help her from the great beyond. How do you break this metal without hurting the leg beneath? A sledgehammer? An industrial sized pair of tinsnips? No, the voice of her ancestor bellowed. Get with it! Use your head! Amy mulled this over in her mind for a whole day and night. Then she had an idea. Let them do it. The ones at the home. They had put it on. Let them take it off. But how to make them do it?

A few days later, Amy's heart was beating hard in her chest as she passed once more into the daffy ward. The answer had come to her in the night, made her sit straight up in bed and laugh out loud. The solution to the manacle problem was now in a plastic package in her purse. Twizzlers! Amy knew that Clara loved red licorice. Always had. When they were young, Clara was rarely seen without one hanging from her mouth like a limp red cigarette. On Saturday afternoons at the show when Amy bought popcorn and a drink, Clara armed herself with several packages of

9249* by Mary Haylock

red licorice and often had to go back to the candy counter at intermission for more. One day when they were fifteen, Amy and Clara made their way out of the darkened theatre munching on the remnants of their treats:

"That movie was really good, eh? I just loved Annette Funicello's hair. And Frankie Avalon is dreamy, don't you think Clara?" Amy said. Then she took a good look at her friend in the bright light of the outside world. "Clara! What's wrong with you? You're red all over your face. I think you've got the measles!" Clara was too busy scratching to respond.

The doctor sent Clara for tests at the hospital and they discovered her allergy to many things, chief among them, red licorice. Clara had to give it up. And now, Amy was relying on that old allergy to get Clara out of bondage. Her purse was loaded with enough of the stuff to turn Clara into the Scarlet Pimpernel. Hopefully, the rash would cover her legs and make them take off the anklet to give her some relief from the itching. At that moment, Amy would leap into action. But was Clara still allergic after all these years? And if she was, would she react immediately? If it took too long, Amy wouldn't be there to spirit her away unnoticed. It was a helluva long shot, but worth a try.

Out in the car, Amy's bag was packed with everything they would need for the trip. She'd made up a story for her kids, something about a girly week in Ottawa with her book club. All she had to do was grab a few of Clara's clothes and toiletries and get her out of there before anyone was the wiser. Their two passports were zipped securely into a pocket in Amy's purse. Whatever they didn't have, they could buy on her clean Visa with the ten-thousand-dollar limit. Let the kids pay it back out of their inheritance when she died.

9249 by Mary Haylock*

As usual, Amy found Clara asleep in her bed when she arrived at ten o'clock in the morning. Slowly she came to and sat up at the sound of Amy's voice in her ear:

"Come on, Toots. Rise and shine. We have a busy day today."

"Where are we going?"

"I'd tell you, but you'd never believe me in a million years."

Clara looked at Amy with a curious expression in her eyes.

"Look what I brought you, Amy said. "Your favourite thing on the planet. Red licorice. Remember how you used to love this stuff? Here, have a piece."

For a moment Clara stared at the licorice stick with a puzzled frown, then she looked trustingly at Amy, stuck the candy in her mouth and began to chew. Amy waited and watched. Nothing happened. When Clara had finished chewing, Amy offered her another piece, anxious to see if she would turn red and start to scratch. But Clara just chewed endlessly and finally swallowed without anything untoward happening. She reached for another piece.

"Let's go for a walk," Amy said. Clara linked her arm through Amy's, and they set off down the hall together in companionable silence.

"Where are we going?"

"South, where oranges grow on trees and the gulf breezes blow on the sandy beaches. How would you like that?"

"Yes, but they won't let me."
"Just wait and see, Clarabelle, just wait and see."

9249* by Mary Haylock

They sat on a bench in the enclosed courtyard and watched a cleaning lady go by with her cart. The woman had dark skin. She smiled at them and said hello in a sing-song voice, somewhere from the islands, Jamaica maybe. She and Clara had been to Jamaica back in the good old days. Drank a lot of yellow birds. Smoked a bit of ganga in a little straw hut near the beach with some dark-skinned guys with red eyes. Amy wondered if they liked to be called negro or black or Jamaican/ Canadian or whatever. But she kept quiet about things like this. She knew she wasn't politically correct anymore. She couldn't keep up with the latest trends. Her grandchildren were always giggling behind her back when she said things like, "nigger in the woodpile," or "jewed him down." It was hard when the words just popped out of her mouth. After all, she'd grown up hearing these expressions all her life and now when she was older, they seemed to be right on the tip of her tongue when she spoke. It was better, she learned, to just keep quiet and listen when the younger generation were around. They didn't understand. It was just the way things were back then. They hadn't known any better. It was different when she and Clara were alone. They could say anything they liked and neither of them were offended.

Clara took her hand from Amy's and scratched her arm. Amy was on instant alert. A red patch appeared where Clara's fingers had been. Was it just a coincidence? No. Clara was scratching the end of her nose now and a flush of pink extended on both cheeks from her nose to her hairline. Amy turned in her seat to watch. Clara was turning red, even the whites of her eyes were beginning to look bloodshot like those guys in the ganga hut. Yes! It was happening right before her eyes.

By the time they got back to Clara's room, she was itching all over and Amy knew it was time to look under the anklet. Both legs were red and bumpy down to the top of the ankle socks that Clara wore. Amy peeled back the sock and peeked underneath the bracelet. There was the same rash, looking angry and uncomfortable. While Clara scratched, Amy pushed the buzzer beside the bed. The moment of truth was at hand!

It took several pushes and about twenty minutes before anyone answered the call. By now Clara was sneezing at regular intervals and rolling around on the bed to relieve the intense itching. The attendant who answered the buzzer watched her in growing alarm. Amy didn't know if she was a nurse or an aide or a member of the cleaning staff. The woman turned on her heel and left the room quickly without a word. Amy thought about the old days when the nurses in a hospital were unmistakable. You could tell by the black bands on the starched white hats perched on top of their heads. She remembered Sister Mary Frances, the head of the obstetrics ward where Amy's children had been born almost fifty years ago. In her impeccable white wimple and flowing robe, she commanded respect wherever she went, keeping the members of staff in line with a look and even cowing some visiting doctors with her imperious authority.

In the night one of the women in the ward had started to bleed and Amy awoke to hear the nurses talking. The doctor can't be reached. What are we going to do? At that moment, Sister Mary Frances had swept through the door like an avenging angel, brandishing a shiny metal pan which she handed to one of the nurses to catch the flow of blood.

"What shall we do, sister?" the flustered nurse asked.

"Pack her, of course." Sister Mary Frances didn't hesitate for a moment.

"But Sister, we can't get hold of the doctor. We don't have permission."

"Pack her, I said. I'll worry about the doctor." With that she glided out the door as silently as she had come. Everyone sighed

9249* by Mary Haylock

with relief. In the morning, the girl was sitting up in bed nursing her new baby, pale but alive. All was right with the world.

But where were these people now? Whenever Amy had occasion to be in a hospital, she couldn't tell the doctors from the cleaners, and there was never anyone like Sister Mary Frances in sight. Her kind had been declared redundant. Maybe if she was still there, hospitals wouldn't be in the shape they were in now. And nursing homes too. All those germs and infections. Groups of workers standing around talking about whose turn it was to go on a break while some poor slob on a gurney in the hall gasped out his last breath. Amy couldn't imagine anyone getting away with this while Sister Mary Frances, the scourge of St. Joseph's, patrolled the halls, all-seeing, all-knowing and always unmistakeably in charge.

At last the door of Clara's room opened again and two women came in. One was calm and exuded an air of competence. Amy couldn't read the little plastic picture card attached to her chest, but she was sure she was a nurse.

"Has Mrs. Cunningham ingested anything unusual today?" she said.

Amy tried not to look guilty. She noticed the plastic package of red licorice sticking out of the top compartment of her purse and hoped that the nurse wouldn't see it. Sister Mary Frances most assuredly would have.

"Not that I know of. I just got here, and we went for a little walk down the hall and all of a sudden, she got red and started scratching. We came back here, and she's been getting worse and worse." Amy marvelled at what an accomplished liar she had become.

"I can't understand it. She's been here a long time now so there shouldn't be anything new in her environment unless it was brought in from the outside." The nurse narrowed her eyes and started to look around the room. Amy placed herself in the nurse's line of vision blocking her view of the poisonous licorice poking out of her purse.

"Don't you think you should give her something for the itching? It looks pretty bad and I'm afraid she'll start to bleed soon if she doesn't stop scratching," Amy said.

"We need doctor's permission to give Mrs. Cunningham any medication. It might interfere with her other prescribed meds." She took a blood pressure cuff from the apparatus on the wall and started to wrap it around Clara's arm. It took some doing, since Clara tried to yank it off before the nurse could pump it up. "Now Mrs. Cunningham, just relax. You'll be fine." She calmly held her stethoscope to Clara's arm and listened.

Amy watched Clara writhing on the bed and began to wonder if her plan had been such a good one after all. She hadn't wanted Clara to suffer. Why didn't they just give her an antihistamine and put some salve on the awful red bumps all over her body? The hell with the damned doctor. Where was Sister Mary Frances when she was needed?

9249* by Mary Haylock

Chapter 5

By the time a doctor showed up to have a look at Clara, her symptoms had abated somewhat, and Amy was afraid they would disappear altogether. The doctor prescribed some antihistamine and a salve for Clara's itchy rash, then he headed out the door without speaking to Amy. He didn't seem to notice her. The nurse administered the drug and applied the cream all over Clara's arms and legs and face. Everywhere but under the ankle device. Leaning over the nurse's shoulder, Amy drew her attention to the place, trying to sound casual.

"Don't you think you should take that thing off? That rash will never heal under there if you don't."

"Please sit down. I am looking after it." The nurse did not sound grateful for Amy's advice.

"But I looked under there and it looks really sore. It would be a shame to leave that one spot uncared for, don't you think? Boy, she was really trying to scratch under there before you came in." Fear made Amy persistent. If they didn't take the damn thing off this whole charade would have been in vain.

"I can't remove the device without permission. It's there for Mrs. Cunningham's protection, you know."

"Who has to give this permission?" Amy had a sinking feeling that it was probably the almighty doctor who had just left the room.

"I guess Mr. Randall would be the one in charge of that. He's the manager of this facility and responsible for the safety of the residents."

"Where is he? Let's go get him." Amy could feel a glimmer of hope that this whole operation might be salvaged after all if she could just get hold of the guy.

"I'll see if he's in," the nurse reluctantly agreed, glaring at Amy as she closed her industrial sized pot of salve and got up from the edge of the bed.

"Good idea, nurse. You really are an angel of mercy." Now please God let Mr. Randall be there. After the nurse left the room, Amy took a straw from the glass of water beside Clara's bed and stuck it under the metal ankle bracelet, causing Clara to moan and scratch where Amy had been poking. She had been almost asleep as the antihistamine took effect and the soothing balm that the nurse applied had started to ease the itching. No use letting Clara get too comfortable. Mr. Randall would need a good reason to take off the cuff. By the time the nurse returned with a young man in tow, Amy's poking had Clara scratching madly around the area of the ankle bracelet, turning the adjacent skin bright red.

Mr. Randall was about eighteen years old, by Amy's calculation. He looked quite a bit like her grandson Derek who was away at college studying basket weaving or some other ridiculous subject. Amy had tried to convince him to choose a profession, but he paid no attention to her, choosing instead a few bird courses that would allow him to continue his extravagant and irresponsible lifestyle unencumbered by the inconvenience of acquiring knowledge of anything worthwhile. Obviously, Mr. Randall's grandmother had been more successful with him since somehow, at his tender age, he was the manager of a large and profitable business. He looked askance at Clara's leg and immediately set about to remove the device, much to Amy's delight. She didn't need to pull out the big guns and suggest that she would convince Clara's daughters to sue Spring Garden Manor claiming elder abuse if he didn't take the thing off. In a few minutes of fussing about with some kind of electronic device, the offensive object lay on Clara's bedside table and Clara's leg was free. Soon after, Mr. Randall went back to his office for his afternoon nap, Amy figured, and the nurse left to solve some other medical crisis in another area of the building. They were alone.

Amy let Clara snooze for a while and then the attendant came to take her to the dining room for lunch. Amy went with her and sat nearby nibbling on a red licorice stick while Clara ate. The food smelled good, some kind of Italian dish, and Clara ate quite a bit before the guy beside her reached over and took the roll from her plate. Clara rose up in her chair and pushed him away.

"Get away from me, you crazy bastard!" Clara yelled. The man cowered in his wheelchair, obviously fearing for his life. Amy was surprised. Clara was uncharacteristically cranky today. Probably as a result of all that scratching. Oh well, Amy smiled a secretive little smirk. Clara would soon be out of here and on her way back to being her old self.

After lunch was over, Amy collected Clara's coat and gloves from the closet and took her back to her room. Clara immediately lay down on the bed and closed her eyes. Amy took this opportunity to clean out the drawers in the dresser and grab some toiletries from the bathroom along with a couple of new rolls of toilet paper. You never know. She shoved everything into the large expandable net grocery sack she carried in her purse. At the last minute she took the half empty jar of salve from the nightstand

and tossed it in. Clara should stop itching soon, but who knows. It was better to be prepared.

When she was done, Amy went to the bathroom and looked at herself in the mirror over the sink. The harsh light showed up all her wrinkles and the dark circles under her eyes which had a kind of wild look. To tell the truth, she looked a bit crazy. I am crazy, she thought. Just as crazy as Clara. I should have my head read for doing this.

But it was too late to back out now. She owed it to her friend to get her out while the getting was good. And what did she have to lose? Her kids were okay, the grandchildren all grown up and no one really needed her anymore. No one but Clara. It felt good to be needed.

"Clara, honey. Wake up. It's time to go."

"Where are we going?" Clara mumbled sleepily and tried to roll over facing the wall.

"Oh no you don't. We've come this far. There's no turning back now. Get up. We're busting out of this joint."

Amy took her to the bathroom and then dressed her in the coat and gloves. She brushed Clara's matted hair and dabbed some lipstick on her pale lips. At the last minute she outlined her own lips in pink. Amy thought they looked pretty good for a pair of old broads on a jail break. Clara smiled coyly at her reflection and started to sing *I Feel Pretty* in a Puerto Rican accent:

"Okay Maria, let's go," Amy said.

It was eerily quiet in the hall. This was the time of day when the residents had their afternoon naps and the staff disappeared for a smoke break out behind the building. The dining room was

9249* by Mary Haylock

empty as Amy pushed the numbers to open the door and led Clara out into Tulipville. A different woman was at the front desk talking on the phone and didn't look up when they walked past. Amy pushed 1...2...3...4...* and opened the outside door, pulling Clara through before she could protest. The silence was deafening. No alarms, no people running, nothing. They were out and no one had even noticed. Amy didn't stop to sign the book. To hell with them. Let them try to find her. They'd never think to look at the border. And by the time anyone realized that they were gone, they'd be halfway to Erie Pennsylvania. Amy's heart was beating hard as she loaded Clara into the car and did up her seatbelt.

"Where are we going?" The pale blue eyes so close to Amy's face looked worried.

This time it was Amy who leaned forward and planted a kiss on Clara's cheek.

"We're going home, Clara. Home where we belong."

"Oh good. It's been so long. Fred will be hungry."

Amy was surprised at the mention of poor Fred. Clara's beloved cat had been dead for two years and Clara hadn't spoken of him for a long time. The girls suspected that Clara had fed him rat poison instead of Mr. Whiskers, but no one knew for sure why he suddenly keeled over and died. Amy and Clara had buried Fred in Clara's rose garden beneath a little ceramic cat to mark the spot.

"Don't worry. We'll get Fred some good old Lake Erie perch for his supper," Amy said.

"Oh, he'll love that." Clara smiled and settled back in the seat.

9249* by Mary Haylock

Amy turned on the motor and eased out of the parking space slowly in case someone was hiding in her blind spot. She couldn't turn her head around too far anymore, so had to rely on her rear-view mirror, which often failed to register baby buggies or old men with canes shuffling by. Safely out on the road at last, Amy began to think about the enormity of what she was doing. Could she still look after the two of them as she had during their travels? She was a lot older now. What if something happened to her? What would become of Clara then? She almost turned around and went back. But then she pictured Clara locked up for life in that Tower of Doom, and she kept going.

Later, as she guided the PT Cruiser down the on ramp into the Niagara bound lanes of the Queen Elizabeth Way with Clara belted into the seat beside her, head back against the headrest, peacefully asleep, Amy smiled. A piece of cake, she thought. We're on our way to the US of A. *No problemo*! Her foot tramped down on the accelerator and shot them out into the bustling afternoon traffic. Amy always closed her eyes when she attempted this manoeuvre. She knew if she saw those big eighteen wheelers bearing down on her she'd never have the nerve to merge. What you don't see can't hurt you, was Amy's motto. All you have to do is close your eyes and put the pedal to the metal. If you're going fast enough, you can squeeze into an invisible space. Gord had told her that when he taught her to drive sixty years ago, and so far, it had always worked just fine.

Swinging at last into the slow lane of the highway where the younger impatient drivers wouldn't bug her, Amy started to relax. They were bringing up the rear of the wagon train, a couple of hardy pioneers heading for the land of the free and the home of the brave.

Clara woke up and began singing along to the music on the radio. It was *The Sunny Side of the Street*.

Chapter 6

Amy started to perspire as the car inched forward in the long customs line-up waiting to cross the Rainbow Bridge. The Niagara river below churned its way from Lake Erie to Lake Ontario, surging and eddying with the spring runoff as it threw itself against the steep walls of the gorge on either side. Clara was awake and agitated as the river itself. Her eyes were wide open, darting here and there as she looked at the cars beside them, full of strangers.

"Where are we going?" Clara sounded really scared.

"Over the bridge to freedom." Amy tried to project a confidence she didn't really feel.

"What's taking so long? Let's go." Clara began to roll up the edge of her scarf into a tight tube.

"We have to wait for customs. They're going to ask us where we were born. Do you remember?"

"Of course. I was born in the back seat of a taxi on the way to St. Joe's."

Amy had heard the story many times. But she knew this wouldn't cut it at customs.

9249* by Mary Haylock

"Well, just tell them Hamilton. That's all they'll want to know. Just say, Hamilton when they ask you where you were born."

"But I was born halfway down the Jolly Cut in a taxi. I have to tell them the truth or they'll put me back in jail."

"No, they won't. Just say Hamilton. Come on, say it with me. Hamilton." Oh god, this wasn't going to work. Why couldn't she have just stayed asleep?

"Hamilton." Clara repeated obediently. Then she started to cheer the Tiger Cats' well-known football cheer.

She shook her imaginary pompoms at the neighbouring car much to the delight of the kids in the back seat. It had been sixty years since Clara had been a high school cheerleader, but she still had all the moves. Finally, the car in front moved on and they pulled ahead.

Amy's worst nightmare was realized. There was a woman in the booth. Women were notoriously hard-nosed at the border. After all they had to prove they were tougher than the men. The sour-faced guard leaned out of her little glass cage and looked Amy straight in the eye.

"Citizenship?" she barked.

Oh god, no!

"Canadian," Amy said loudly, hoping Clara would catch on. Please Clara, say Canadian don't say Hamilton, Amy prayed.

"And you, Ma'am?" The woman leaned further out peering accusingly at Clara.

9249* by Mary Haylock

Amy sat still and felt her heart hammering in her ears. She thought she'd faint. This was it. The jig was up. Amy could picture herself in that ominous looking stone building over there, naked as a jay bird, being told by some hairy border guard to bend over.

"What is your citizenship, please?" the guard repeated loudly.

"Canadian." Clara smiled pleasantly at the woman.

"Passports," the woman said.

Amy fumbled with the zipper on her purse and produced the documents. The guard looked suspiciously at Amy, whose hands were shaking so hard she could hardly hang on to the little folders as she passed them out the window.

"Are you all right Ma'am?" the guard asked as she came down off her perch and took a step toward the car, hard eyes boring into Amy. Amy opened her mouth, but nothing came out, just a kind of gurgling sound. Clara leaned forward and smiled.

"She's just excited," Clara giggled. "We're going to see Fred. We haven't seen him for a long time. We're going to buy him a fish dinner."

"Okay ladies, enjoy your meal." The woman smiled at Clara, handed back the passports and waved them through. Amy felt herself going limp. Somehow, she managed to put the car in drive and step on the gas. They lurched forward and passed under a large sign that said, 'Welcome to the United States of America.' Clara pointed to it.

"Look. We're in the USA." Clara rose to attention in her seat as far as her seatbelt would allow, saluted the sign and began to sing the American national anthem

Amy looked in the rear-view mirror to find out if anyone was after them, but all she could see was an endless stream of cars in the line up behind her. Ahead was a sign that read 'To Buffalo'. Amy followed the arrow to the stretch of open road marked I-90 as it slowly dawned on her that they were free, thanks to Clara. Amy wanted to get out and kiss the ground.

"We did it, Clara. We made it." Amy was ecstatic. Clara had really come through when she had to. That was the old Clara she remembered.

"Let's go home now." Clara said.

By the time they passed the Peach Street exit leading into Erie Pennsylvania, it was dark, and Amy's stomach was rumbling. She had packed a little lunch in a Styrofoam cooler in the back seat, a few bottles of water and some cheese and crackers and they had opened it at one of the highway rest stations on I- 90 when they stopped to pee. But Clara hadn't eaten anything.

"Come on, Clara," Amy coaxed. "You must be getting hungry."

"I don't like cheese and crackers," Clara said. She was silent and withdrawn. It was all Amy could do to get her to drink some water. She knew that old people got funny when they were dehydrated so she made her take a few sips. God knows Clara was funny enough. Amy took a few swigs herself, just for good measure.

As darkness settled over the countryside Amy decided to stop for the night. She didn't see very well after the sun went down. Another of the perks of old age, cataracts. Thank goodness it hadn't rained because that was the worst, all those rainbows around the oncoming headlights and the windshield wipers her son had told her to replace several months ago squeaking and

9249* by Mary Haylock

streaking across her line of vision. Better to sit it out until morning. She found an exit marked with a motel sign and turned off highway 79 just south of Erie. It was a rural area and they had to travel quite a distance on a two-lane road to the Bide-a-Wee Motel, a rundown one-story building on the outskirts of a little no name hamlet. It was probably a place for the locals to shack up with each other incognito. Amy registered at the desk inside and the clerk behind the counter gave her a long hard stare when she said they were two women travelling together. She didn't like the Norman Bates look of the man, long dark hair falling over his forehead, piercing eyes that could undoubtedly see right through the pretend luggage of any pair of adulterous cheaters.

"We're on our way to a judo convention in Atlanta," Amy volunteered.

"Oh, yeah?" The man seemed unimpressed, forcing Amy to add a few more embellishments to her story.

"Yeah, people don't think that a woman my age could be into that sort of kung-fu stuff, but once a black belt, always a black belt, you know. You never really forget the fundamentals." She made her hands into two deadly weapons and took a swipe at the air between them.

"Room 19. Down this way on the left-hand side. It's a double. Is that okay?" He raised one eyebrow.

"Sure. Are there any restaurants around here?"

"Piggly Wiggly down the street has sandwiches sometimes. Check out by eleven."

"Okay. Thanks." Amy signed the credit card bill and picked up the key. "Goodnight then." The man had gone back to reading his paper and didn't respond. Amy hoped she'd intimidated him enough that he wouldn't attempt to murder them in the night. She knew one thing; she wasn't going to take a shower. When she got back to the car, Clara was agitated and trying to undo her seatbelt.

"Where are we going?" She looked at Amy warily as if she'd never seen her before.

"We're going to stay here tonight. Come on. Help me find number 19."

It was at the end of the long low structure, far away from the road. Good, Amy thought. Now the State Police won't see our license plates so easily when they come looking for us.

As she unloaded the suitcases from the car, Amy wondered what was going on at home. By now Mr. Randall would know that one of his captives had flown the coop. Heads would roll. She could just imagine the conversation:

"Who let her out on her own? How the hell did she get through the security door?" Stress would cause Mr. Randall's acne to flare up and set him to scratching the ugly red bumps on his neck.
"You took off her alarm device, Sir." The nurse was not about to take the blame.
"Oh, yes. Well how did she get past the front desk? Who was on duty? I want to know the slacker's name."
"It's a volunteer, Mr. Randall. Her name is Anna. Please don't yell at her, she's already very upset."
"She's upset? What about me? What about the reputation of the Manor? We've never lost anyone before that Cunningham woman came here. It's that sneaky friend of hers. She's the troublemaker. When we find her, she'll be in big trouble and Clara Cunningham will be out on her ear!"

9249* by Mary Haylock

"Don't you think we should call the police and inform Mrs. Cunningham's daughters? She's been missing now for five hours."

"Let's wait just a bit longer, nurse. I hear that goofy friend of hers likes to take her out drinking. Maybe they're getting drunk somewhere and they'll turn up before bedtime."

"Okay, Mr. Randall. You're the boss. But she's missed her meds at dinner time. She'll be getting pretty hard to handle by now, wherever she is.

"I know, I know." Mr. Randall started to nibble at the fingernail on his right index finger. "Oh god, Grandma will kill me when she finds out."

Amy felt a distinct pleasure as she imagined his anxiety. But the meds business really was a concern. Amy didn't know how Clara would react to going off cold turkey like this. But hell, that's how they'd both quit smoking one day when they were forty. Clara had more willpower than Amy who couldn't imagine never smoking again.

"I can't do it, Clara. I feel like I've lost my best friend." Amy said.

"I'm your best friend. And you can do it, Amy. Let's make a pact." Clara had linked her little finger through Amy's. "When we're eighty we'll buy a carton of Du Mauriers and smoke our brains out. Until then, we'll just do without. What do you say?

Somehow it had made it easier for Amy to think about quitting. After all it wasn't forever, it was just forty years. "Okay. I can do that. You're on." And she had done it. No smokes for thirty-five years now. Amy knew deep down that Clara had saved her life. Now it was her turn. It might be hard, but she would help Clara kick the zombie drugs and become herself again. She owed her that much.

9249* by Mary Haylock

It had been a long day, and after sharing a pork on a bun at the Piggly Wiggly deli counter Amy and Clara came straight back to the room and got ready for bed. Clara stood obedient as a child while Amy took off her clothes and pulled the nightgown she'd brought from the Manor over her head. She noticed that Clara's rash had subsided to a pink blush on the areas of skin that she had scratched. Amy managed to convince Clara to pee but didn't bother to get her to clean her teeth, just tucked her into her side of the double bed. Amy was too tired even to put in her eyedrops. She got herself into her pyjamas and turned out the light after locking the door and checking it several times. It was comforting to feel Clara snuggled up to her back and she fell asleep as soon as her head hit the pillow.

Amy didn't know what it was that made her open her eyes. It was dark in the room, but she could see a menacing gray shape standing beside the bed on her side. Her heart began to pound. It was Norman come to murder them. The shape didn't move for what seemed like forever to Amy. She lay perfectly still, gathering her strength until suddenly she made a lunge for him, wrapping her arms around his body so he couldn't stab her with his knife.

"Ow," yelled Clara. "What did you do that for?"

"God, Clara, is that you?" Amy felt the small shape in the nightdress with her hands. "What the hell are you doing? You scared the shit out of me, sneaking up on me like that." Amy went to the door and found the light switch in the darkness. She turned it on and glared at Clara. "How long have you been standing there like that?"

"I can't sleep."

"Why not? You must be tired after the day we've had."

"The freight train."

9249* by Mary Haylock

"What freight train?" Amy wondered if the motel was near a track and she had been so fast asleep that she hadn't heard it.

"Right in here," Clara said, pointing at Amy's side of the bed. "I heard it."

Oh shit! It was her snoring that had wakened Clara, who was a light sleeper. On their travels Clara had always brought earplugs so she could sleep in the same room with Amy. Although she'd never heard it herself, Amy had been told often enough about the way she could 'saw logs'. Poor Gord! He had complained about it for many years. After he died, when people said they hoped he would 'Rest in peace', they didn't realize how right they were.

"Oh, honey. I'm sorry. That was just me snoring."

Clara continued to stand beside the bed staring at Amy's pillow. Amy didn't know what to do. She hadn't thought about keeping Clara awake all night. Somehow, she'd have to improvise some earplugs. She rolled up a couple of Kleenex tissues and shoved them into Clara's ears as far as they would go. Clara looked like a demented bunny rabbit, with droopy white ears on either side of her head.

"Okay, Flopsy. Let's hit the sack. No more freight trains, I promise."

Clara pulled out the Kleenex wads. "What did you say?"

"Nothing. Let's go to sleep. Okay?" Amy stuffed the tissues back in Clara's ears and pulled the blanket up around her neck. She closed her eyes and rested her head on her hands, miming what she wanted Clara to do. Clara closed her eyes and pretended to be asleep as Amy turned out the light. Amy lay down on her side of the bed and vowed to stay awake until Clara was really asleep. Oh boy, she thought. It's going to be a long night.

It seemed like forever that Amy kept herself awake, feeling herself drifting off and then making a monumental effort to pull herself back from oblivion. The clock on the nightstand said three o'clock and still Amy wasn't sure if Clara was really sleeping or not. At last, though, Amy was so tired she couldn't stay awake any longer. She allowed herself to let go and drift away into dreamland. And what dreams they were, people chasing her and finding her escape route obstructed no matter where she turned. Terrifying, frustrating no way out dreams where some unimaginable danger lurked around every corner. Gord was in the dream, at least it seemed like him, but always just a little ahead of her. He wouldn't slow down or turn around to wait for her. And Mr. Randall also appeared, fishing in a lake, using red licorice worms for bait. But the worst apparition was when Amy rolled over in bed and instead of Clara's sweet familiar face, she saw the customs woman leering at her. She couldn't breathe. She tried, but the woman was lying on top of her, crushing the air out of her lungs.

With a snort, Amy woke up and felt the pillow over her face, being pressed down on her by that horrible woman. But no, it wasn't her. And it wasn't a dream. Amy was wide awake now and struggling to push a very real pillow off her face. With a burst of adrenaline, she managed to get her head out from under and found herself looking into Clara's eyes. Mad, wild eyes.

"Shut up, shut up, shut up!" Clara yelled as she staggered back from the bed and dropped the pillow to the floor. Amy gasped for breath.

"You tried to kill me, Clara! How could you?" Amy felt the tears starting up. Clara just stared at her in silence. Then she went back to her side of the bed and crawled in. She closed her eyes and immediately Amy heard the sound of deep breathing. Clara was asleep.

Holy shit, Amy thought. What have I got myself into? To think I was worried about Norman Bates. I've got Clara the Exterminator right beside me in bed.

9249* by Mary Haylock

9249* by Mary Haylock

Chapter 7

When Amy woke up next morning, Clara was nowhere to be found. Not in the bathroom, not under the bed or in the closet. In an absolute panic, Amy threw on her clothes and ran to the office. Clara was sitting in the window with a strange woman, probably Norman's day shift replacement. When Clara caught sight of Amy she waved and motioned for her to come in. The woman stood up and let Amy have the empty chair.

Clara picked up a half empty mug from the table between the two chairs and took a sip. Obviously, she had been here a while.

"Would you like some coffee?" the woman asked. "It's free for guests of the motel."

"Yes, thank you. I'd like a coffee." Amy felt a bit weak in the knees. Thank god Clara was here. She could have been anywhere, on the road, lost in the woods nearby. God only knew how long she'd been out, with Amy snoring away in bed. Some caretaker I am, Amy thought. Visions of Mr, Randall's disapproving face danced in her imagination.

"You're a lazybones." Clara smiled at her and then at the woman, who nodded. Obviously they were in cahoots.

"Thanks for looking after her, I mean the coffee and all," Amy said. The woman handed her a steaming cup and she took a big gulp.

"Not at all, dear," the woman replied. "We had quite a nice conversation. It gets lonely here sometimes. It's just me and Harold now the kids are away at college in Pittsburgh. I really enjoyed talking to your friend here. She wouldn't tell me her name, though. She seems a bit shy with strangers. The woman gave Amy a quizzical look as she patted Clara on the shoulder. Thank god Clara hadn't been in a talkative mood. She might have blown the whistle on both of them.

"She's Thelma and I'm Louise," Amy said boldly. No use making it too easy for the cops when they came calling. Then she remembered that she had used their real names when she signed the register last night. She tried to backtrack a little. "We have two names actually, I'm Thelma Amy and she's Louise Clara." Amy hoped this would allay any suspicions the woman may have acquired from her conversation with Clara. God knows what they had talked about.

The woman frowned and glanced at the register open on the desk in front of her, but she didn't comment. "Well, I'd better get to work. Beds to make, toilets to clean." Her hands were red and scratchy looking. "I get the fun stuff to do in the daytime. Harold gets to watch tv at night."

"Isn't that just the way," Amy commiserated with the woman, trying to finish her coffee and get out of there before their cover was blown. To Amy's surprise Clara chimed in too.

"Yes, that's just like my Fred. What a messy animal he is. Food all over the floor and litter scattered everywhere. I could just kill him." The woman nodded in sympathy.

9249* by Mary Haylock

You did kill him, Amy thought. "Well, thanks for the coffee," she said. We'll be on our way now. Maybe we'll stop in again on our way back. You've been very nice. Come on Louise. Let's go." She took Clara's hand and opened the door.

"Where are we going?' asked Clara looking thoroughly confused. Amy pulled the door shut behind them and marched her back to room 19. That had been a close call. She had to get Clara out of there quick before the woman started to think about the strange pair who had spent the night. She might just put in a call to the State troopers. Amy could just imagine that conversation too:

Hello, is that you Donna? It's me, Wanda, out at the Bide-a-wee motel on Route three?... Yes, he's doing fine down there at the college. Thanks. How's Lavonia doing in hairdressing school?... Oh, good for her. I'll have to pop in and get a do one of these days.

Say, Donna. I had kind of a strange pair at the motel last night.... No, not that! These were two women, Canadians, by the license plate on their car. They were going south to Florida. It seemed kinda strange to me, when all the other snowbirds are heading north at this time of year.... Oh, I know. They're a strange bunch up there. I guess it snows most of the time, so they just want to get out and go where it's warm. But the thing is, Donna, they were really weird....

Well, one of them was okay, she was quite nice, but the other one bossed her around and made up phoney names for them and stuff like that. She sure was in a hurry to get out of here. What do you make of that?... I thought it might be a kidnapping or something 'cause the little one just kept saying she wanted to go home....

No, no, they were both old ladies, but one of them just acted really suspicious.... I don't know, maybe Joe should come out here and talk to Harold. Would you mind asking him if he has time?... Thanks Donna. I'm likely all wet, but that big one really bugged me somehow....

Okay then. Bye-bye.

Clara sat on the bed while Amy packed their belongings into the little carry-on bag and straightened up the room. She left the key on the makeshift desk in the corner. She didn't want to encounter the woman again. Then they were off down the little country road back to the highway where they had a choice, 79 north or 79 south. Amy wondered if she should take the northern route back home. She hadn't had much sleep and could feel a headache creeping up the back of her neck. And she had really been terrible at looking after Clara. Maybe she'd bitten off more than she could chew. She glanced at her companion and Clara smiled back.

"What are we waiting for?" Clara said.

That was all Amy needed to hear. "Okay kiddo. Here we go."

Amy took the bypass around Pittsburgh and continued on through the rolling countryside of Pennsylvania watching the greening of the trees and fields as they headed due south. Whenever she spotted a police car, she made sure she wasn't speeding and held her breath until it passed her. But she didn't think the ones at home would have figured out where they'd gone yet. The kids would know they were missing though, and Amy hoped they wouldn't be too worried. At least they'd figure out that they were together and that would make them feel better. Clara's girls would relax a bit when they knew Amy was with her. And Amy's boys would say what a pain in the ass their mother was, but secretly they'd admire her adventurous spirit. They knew she could look after herself.

9249* by Mary Haylock

Clara dozed on and off during the afternoon hours, rousing herself once in a while to ask where they were going, but sometimes not staying awake long enough to hear Amy's reply. They had lunch at a Denny's restaurant but once again Clara didn't eat much, and Amy had to force her to drink something. Her face was starting to look drawn and pinched. By three in the afternoon, Amy was struggling to stay awake herself. The road was straight and there wasn't much traffic as the little car drifted up and down the hills getting closer and closer to the state line. Finally, Amy knew she had to stop for a while. She pulled into a rest stop and they went inside to use the facilities.

As soon as they stepped inside the door, they were met by a group of strangers who swept them into the main room of the large cedar building. It was obviously a welcome centre. She must have missed the border signs when they passed out of Pennsylvania. Cameras snapped pictures of the two startled women, and everyone was talking at once. Oh god, Amy thought, they've caught us. But these weren't cops, they were people in park ranger uniforms laughing and patting them on the back. A large important-looking man in a suit pulled them along to a platform where a tv camera was pointed in their direction.

"Congratulations, little ladies," he exclaimed heartily. "You are the one millionth visitors to the magnificent state of West Virginia to pass through our new welcome centre. We have a nice surprise for you. Now, where are you ladies from?"

"Hamilton," Clara said, smiling at the camera and waving.

"And where might that be, little lady?" He gave Clara's shoulder a squeeze and she peeked up at him fluttering her eyelashes.

"Canada," Amy interjected quickly before Clara had a chance to tell her 'born in a taxi' story.

"Well, well, a couple of Canucks have won our prize, folks. Isn't that nice. The sovereign state of West Virginia welcomes you ladies. And in the name of Governor Jacob Statler it is my distinct pleasure to award you this cheque in the amount of one thousand dollars." Everyone applauded politely.

Amy tried to hide her face behind the man as Clara stepped forward and took hold of one corner of a large piece of cardboard made to look like a cheque.

"Thank you," Clara said, nodding and smiling as the camera rolled.

"Enjoy your stay with us ladies," the man said as he shook Amy's hand and showed all his teeth in a broad grin. Then he turned to Clara and started to explain what to do with the big cheque. She frowned and held on tightly to the corner of it.

"Now where are you two headed, may I ask?" He tried gently to remove Clara's fingers from the phoney cheque.

"To see Fred," Clara replied politely as she jerked it back out of his hand. "He's waiting for his fish."

"Well you came to the right place, dear. The sovereign state of West Virginia is known as the land of the mighty rainbow. Best trout streams in this beautiful land of ours. Now you take the Monongahela. There's a river just jumpin' with the biggest fish you ever did see." He gave up on the cheque and faced the camera with a toothy smile.

Amy seemed to recall that the sovereign state of West Virginia was better known for its coal mines and unemployment than trout fishing. One thing she knew for sure, though, they had to get out of there. "Sorry, chief," Amy interrupted. "We really have to use your beautiful facilities if you don't mind. That's why we pulled in here."

"Of course, of course," he blustered as Amy whisked Clara away in the direction of the washroom after prying the artificial cheque out of her hand.

My God, Amy thought. What were the odds of being singled out like this when all they wanted was anonymity? Their pictures would be plastered all over Coalville, West Virginia where the camera originated, according to the sign on the side of it, WVBC Coalville. She doubted that anyone in Hamilton would see it, though. And what about the cheque? They sure could use the money but was it worth it to leave a paper trail like that? Amy didn't think so. There was an exit door in the washroom leading to the outside. Amy grabbed Clara's hand and they left as quietly as they could. Hopefully, if the reception committee tried to follow them, they'd look north in the direction most Canadians were travelling at this time of year and not south.

Back on the road, Amy was wide awake now, and nervous. Every flashing light, every police car made her break out in a sweat. After several hours, they saw a large sign ahead. Welcome to Virginia, it said. There was another welcome centre, but this time Amy passed on by. This one could be booby trapped like the last one. Once they got past that, Amy started to relax a bit and look for a place to stop for dinner. She was worried about Clara, who hadn't eaten much of anything since they left home. She was staring straight ahead and hadn't said anything for many miles. Even the songs on the radio didn't elicit a response from her. Her eyes had a scary blank look.

"There's a Howard Johnson's, Clara. Do you want to try that for supper?" Amy slowed down and swung the car onto the exit ramp leading to the restaurant. Clara didn't respond. When Amy opened the passenger door and reached across to undo her seatbelt Clara sat perfectly still.

"Come on, honey. Let's get some grub." Without warning, Clara punched her in the shoulder and started to yell.

"No! No! I don't want to go. You can't make me. Get away from me. I don't know you!" Her eyes were wild, and her face was screwed up into a mask of fear and hatred as she continued to flail at Amy with both fists. Amy backed away and slammed the car door. Fortunately, she hadn't undone the seatbelt. Clara continued to rock the car with her violent motions as she tried to get at Amy through the glass, hands curled into two claws, lips drawn back to show her teeth, like some animal in a cage. Amy was horrified. She'd never seen Clara like this. Not ever, even when they were young. She didn't know what to do. Just as suddenly as it began, Clara's tirade ended. She hung forward in the seatbelt breathing hard, but quiet and looking more like herself now.

"Holy shit!" Amy said out loud. "What the hell was that all about?" She looked up to see several people inside the restaurant peering out the window at her with concern in their eyes. This was likely not a good place to stop for supper. She got back into the car, watching her companion stealthily out of the corner of her eye, ready to duck if she had to. They headed once more for the open road.

9249* by Mary Haylock

Chapter 8

After her outburst Clara subsided into her zombie state and Amy was left on her own with nothing to do but think. She had heard that Alzheimer's patients sometimes became violent, but she had never really believed that Clara could be capable of such behaviour. Obviously she had been wrong. Her shoulder was still aching from the blows Clara had inflicted.

Little Clara. But she had always been strong for her size. Nurses had to have muscles to hoist their patients around, sometimes men twice as big as they were. 'Mighty Mouse', Gord used to call Clara. He liked her shoulder massages better than the ones he got from Amy. They were like butterfly farts he said, compared to Clara's strong hands digging into his sore muscles. Nurse's hands that knew where the sinews and tendons were. After their usual Sunday game of golf at Sunnibreeze in Florida he'd sit in a kitchen chair while Clara stood behind him working away until she'd loosened up all the knots in his arthritic shoulders. Amy would make brunch and they'd all eat bacon and eggs and laugh about their lousy games. For her size, Clara could smack that big driver of hers into the ball and set it sailing a long way. Trouble was, it didn't always go the way she wanted it to.

Amy wondered if Clara would still be able to play golf. She hoped swinging a club would have become an automatic reflex and it would all come back to her somehow. Surely something repetitive like that would be ingrained in the muscles. Clara's body would remember for her. It would be great to get out on the course again. Amy hadn't played since Clara left her. There were lots of good little par three courses where they were headed in Florida. It would be fun to get out in the fresh air and play again.

Then again, maybe Clara wouldn't be able to do the things they used to do anymore. Amy thought about what happened the last time she took Clara to the casino. It was at the end of the summer, their final adventure together before Clara got 'put away'. Amy had rented a cottage up north for a few weeks in August and on Clara's seventy-fifth birthday, they had driven to the nearby casino in Orillia to celebrate. Clara seemed to have forgotten how to play the slots. They sat down, side by side, and Amy put a twenty-dollar bill into Clara's machine.

"There. Twenty-five lines at one cent a line," Amy had said in her best schoolteacher voice. "Now just push this button that says 'spin' and see what happens."

Clara obeyed Amy's instructions. When the reels stopped Clara sat still with her hands in her lap staring at the brightly lit screen in front of her.

"Push the button again, Clara," Amy said.

"I can't. It says, 'game over'."

"Well, that just means that part of the game. You can still play. Push it again."

"Okay." Amy could tell that Clara didn't really believe her. She looked surprised when the reels turned. When they stopped, Clara again sat with her hands in her lap, looking at the machine.

"Do it again, Clara."

"I can't."

"Why not?" Amy's patience was wearing thin.

"It says, 'game over'."

"It's not over yet. Do it again." It was hard to keep the irritation out of her voice.

"Okay." Clara looked at Amy like she was nuts. The reels tumbled erratically and then stopped. Bells started to ring showing that Clara had won the bonus feature, fifteen free spins. Clara started to push the button again.

"No, you don't have to push the button now. It'll go on its own. Just sit there."

"Okay." Clara watched with her hands in her lap as the flashing images changed over and over again all on their own. She didn't notice her total amount of money growing. The twenty dollars Amy had put into the machine had now become forty-nine. When it stopped again the screen lit up with a sign that said, 'Congratulations'. Clara smiled and sat very still.

Meanwhile, Amy had run out of money and put another twenty into the slot of her own machine.

"Keep playing, Clara. You won. Look up there. You won twenty-nine dollars." Clara clapped her hands in delight and continued to sit.

"Push the button," Amy ordered. Clara pushed and Amy turned her attention to her own machine. Her luck was lousy tonight. No big wins at all. Then the machine beside her went crazy. Horns blared, lights flashed, the sound of money hitting metal echoed in her ears. Clara had hit the jackpot! And it was the major prize, the biggest one, the one you had to be playing all the lines and the maximum amount of money to be eligible to win. Clara must have hit the wrong button, the one that said, 'Max Bet'. The screen lit up with fireworks and a brass band was playing. Clara had won fifteen hundred dollars!

An attendant came and placed fifteen crisp hundred-dollar bills into Clara's hand. Clara opened her purse and stuffed them in. Everyone around them applauded. When the excitement was over, Amy turned her attention back to her own machine. She still had twelve dollars in there. She pushed the button quickly several times while Clara sat quietly beside her, staring at her screen. Then she started to pound on the 'spin' button with her fist.

"Clara, stop. What's the matter?"

"It has my money in there."

"It just gave you way more than you put in. It doesn't owe you anything."

"I want my money back. It took my money." Clara started to smack her open hand on the front of the machine. "Give me my money, you Sucker."

Amy got up quickly and guided the irate Clara to the washroom and then to the parking lot outside. The fresh air seemed to cool her off and she took Amy's arm as they walked back to the car.

"That was fun, Amy. I won, didn't I?"

"You sure did, kiddo. It cost me sixty bucks though. Do you want to give me some of your winnings?"

9249* by Mary Haylock

"No way," Clara laughed and clutched her purse tighter to her side.

When they got home the money was nowhere to be found. They dumped the purse and looked in all the secret compartments, even the lining. Amy made Clara empty her pockets and even peeked into her underwear. They both stashed things in their cleavage sometimes, in 'the vault', things like grocery lists and tissues. Nothing was found.

Amy called the casino and made a futile request that someone look in the washroom where they had gone before they left. According to the voice on the phone the money hadn't been turned in and the person sounded doubtful that it would ever be found. That was that. Fifteen hundred dollars down the toilet, maybe literally. Amy was upset, but Clara just smiled secretively. She liked to hide things in places where they would never be found.

As Amy remembered this outing, she realized that Clara had indeed shown signs of unreasonable anger several times before this incident just a while ago in the restaurant parking lot. For a while these flare-ups had seemed to be escalating in frequency but after Clara had gone to Spring Garden Manor, the outbursts happened less often. The medication she was on must have calmed her down and kept Clara's anger under control. But now that Clara was drug free, what would happen? For the second time Amy was afraid maybe she had taken on more than she could handle.

By the time they hit the outskirts of Charlotte North Carolina, the traffic was so congested that Amy didn't have time to worry about much else. Clara dozed on and off while Amy clutched the wheel and wove her way through the maze of overpasses and underpasses, trying to make out signs that came up more quickly than she could read them, sending her lurching from lane to lane

9249* by Mary Haylock

across eight lanes of vehicles to get to the right exit. Several cars honked at them rudely and swerved around her car as they slowed down so as not to miss the cut-off to South Carolina. Clara woke up long enough to give one of them the finger.

After what seemed like hours, the traffic thinned out and they found themselves on a quiet two-lane road leading down from the foothills of the high country. Amy had to pry her fingers from the steering wheel. She left wet marks on the plastic where her hands had hung on for dear life. It was really warm now and humid. On the far side of Charlotte, they saw subdivisions of beautiful new homes created in the image of Gone with the Wind, miniature plantations with tall white columns holding up little second story balconies dripping with colourful wisteria blooms.

Further on they passed through farm country and small towns that were all but deserted in the afternoon sun. Frame buildings along a little street that had been there since confederate times, unpainted and unoccupied by anything but the very old black folk she saw rocking on their porches, waiting among the azaleas for something to bring them back to life. Sometimes half hidden by moss in a little stand of woods at the edge of a farmer's field Amy caught a glimpse of decrepit log buildings that looked like they might have been slave quarters in the old days. She thought about the horror of human beings being treated so cruelly, manacled to prevent them from running away and whipped when they were dragged back by the slave hunters to a life of degradation and tears. At least Clara wouldn't be whipped if they got caught. But that manacle of hers really bothered Amy. It just wasn't right somehow for any human being to be shackled that way. She started to feel justified in what she had done, a sort of modern-day Harriet Tubman, rescuing Clara from a life of slavery.

Chapter 9

The next day they were on the road again after an uneventful night in a Day's Inn motel. Clara had seemed very tired when they arrived last night and had fallen asleep immediately. Amy waited until she was sure Clara was really dead to the world before she slipped into bed and turned out the light. She slept lightly, waking up at the slightest creak of the floorboards or sound of water running in the pipes next door. Finally, as the blackness of the room began to turn grey in the early morning hours Amy fell into a deeper sleep. She woke to see Clara rummaging in her suitcase which lay open on the floor. Amy watched for a while, but she couldn't make much sense of what Clara was doing. She'd take something out, fold it carefully and put it right back where it had been before. Amy sat up in bed and turned on the light.

"What are you looking for, Clara?"

"I can't find it," Clara said. She sounded worried.

"What can't you find?"

"I don't know."

"Why don't you go back to sleep and we'll look for it in the morning."

"What will we look for?"

9249 by Mary Haylock*

"I don't know. You're the one who's lost something."

"What did I lose?"

"I don't freakin' know." Amy tried to keep her tone of voice under control, but she felt like she was in the middle of an Abbot and Costello skit.

"Here it is," Clara pulled her hairbrush out of the suitcase for the third time and looked pleased with herself. Then she put it back, closed the lid and crawled back into bed. In a few minutes she was breathing heavily with her mouth open. Amy lay back against the pillow wide awake now and wondering what to do with herself. She decided to get up and make an early start. She was too excited to go back to sleep. They would be leaving North Carolina soon and heading into South Carolina, the beginning of the real south.

Once they got rolling Clara seemed just fine. She even ate a bit of the ham and egg breakfast that Amy ordered for her in the motel restaurant. Clara laughed when the waitress said, "Y'all want grits with yer coffee?"

"Sho do, Honey chile," Clara said. She even ate a few of them after Amy doctored them up with butter and salt. Then she made a face and pushed her plate away.

"Cream of wheat." she said in disgust.

After they had driven a while the signs told Amy they were in South Carolina, and so did the weather. Spring was in full bloom everywhere along the highway. Forsythia branches bent double from the weight of their yellow blossoms and the grass was green and covered with early morning dew. It was hard to believe that only two days ago they had been wearing winter coats. Clara

9249* by Mary Haylock

started to sing along with the radio again and Amy joined in with her, their voices blending happily in Carolina in the Morning.

Amy began to feel good about their escape. She could tell that Clara was better already. And the police who passed them just smiled at the two little old ladies in the purple PT Cruiser tooling along at the speed limit, singing their hearts out. Clara waved at everyone who passed them and even the cops waved back. Little did they know they were looking at two escaped fugitives from Ontario, Amy thought, feeling a rush of excitement. She hadn't felt this daring in ages. Imagine being on the lam at her age. She pictured herself with big Joan Crawford shoulders, holding a cigarette between her scarlet lips and letting the smoke drift up into her eyes like Lauren Bacall.

Catch me if you can, flatfoot!

As they crossed the Georgia state line that afternoon, Amy could feel the damp heat seeping into her skin. The road rumbled over bridges spanning the miles of swamp land near the coast. The sea air was pleasant except for the odd paper mill that billowed out its foul odour in their direction. Amy didn't want to think about how many miles of toilet paper the mill had cranked out since last time she was here, polluting the air in Georgia and the water in the rest of the country. When she and Clara had been in Greece, they had at first been shocked by the toilet habits of the Greeks who didn't put soiled paper into the toilets. Instead they used a waste container beside the toilet. Amy supposed it then went to a landfill site somewhere and that was bad, but somehow the waters around the Greek islands were clear and unpolluted even after all these centuries of habitation. You could see your toes when you went swimming in the Aegean Sea. The Greeks had spread their political theories and their restaurants around the world. Too bad their bathroom habits hadn't caught on. The water here in North America might be in better shape.

9249* by Mary Haylock

Amy had always fancied herself more than a bit of an environmentalist. She had managed to have a little compost heap at the back of her garden wherever she lived, and she collected rainwater in an old whiskey barrel shoved under the drainpipe. But as she got older, it wasn't always so easy to live this way. The compost was hard to turn over with a shovel when your shoulders ached from arthritis and after Gord died she just couldn't do it anymore alone. The rain barrel became a breeding ground for mosquitoes and when she opened the lid of the composter and saw a pale-faced possum hissing at her from among the corn cobs, she closed the lid and left him to it.

Clara kept trying though. She got one of those fancy composters that you turned with a crank, and with her small muscular arms she managed to keep it working well. Her rose garden was always a picture in June, with roses of every colour that she had collected to match the names of her female relatives. Helen for her mother, Debbie for her oldest daughter and Elizabeth and Eloise for her old aunts. There was even an Amy rose, a recent acquisition that Clara proudly showed her when it bloomed for the first time.

"Look at this one, Amy. Isn't it gorgeous? I love the ruffled petals and the wonderful fragrance, don't you?"

"Yes, this is the best one yet. What's the name of this one?" Amy bent over and took a sniff.

"It's an old-fashioned tea rose, and its name is Amy. I love it because it doesn't have any thorns." Clara smiled at her friend with a look of warm affection.

"Thank you, Clara. It's beautiful. I'm honoured to be here with all your ancestors."

9249* by Mary Haylock

Later Clara picked a little bouquet of Amy's namesake roses and brought them to her house. But after a while Clara forgot the names of the roses as well as the names of the women they were meant to represent. In the spring before she was taken to the Manor, all of Clara's roses died. The stems were black and twisted and no buds appeared anywhere. Her daughters speculated that she had put something toxic into the composter and then spread it on the roses, causing their untimely demise. Like Fred, the cat, they rotted in the barren ground of Clara's once beautiful garden.

Back on the road, Clara was singing again along with Ray Charles, never missing a word of *Georgia on My Mind*

They were headed for Savannah now, past roadside stands selling pecans and peach conserves and Claxton fruitcakes. There didn't seem to be as many of them as Amy remembered, probably because of the big box stores cutting into their profits. These little businesses used to thrive along the interstate. They stopped at a place Amy remembered called The Peach Pit. It was a relic of the old days, a shambling wreck of a building with huge bags of pecans piled up on the front porch and barrels set up inside with a variety of preserves in glass jars artistically displayed on red gingham tablecloths. Amy bought two pecan logs for them to eat, just for old time's sake.

Clara seemed to enjoy the sweet treat as they walked out back along a little boardwalk and stopped to stare in wonder at an enormous alligator lying still as death in a small pool of greasy water. The sign beside the display said his name was Albert and he had been caught in 1949 in the Okefenokee swamp. He had been held in this small pen almost as long as Amy had been alive. No one knew how old he really was. His skin was mottled grey and green with mossy patches of seaweed growing on it. He showed no signs of life.

Amy remembered seeing him ten years before when she'd stopped here with Gord. Albert had looked just the same then. It made her sick to think he had been kept imprisoned in that small enclosure for all those years, deprived of his ability to swim freely and associate with others of his own kind. Amy stared hard at him and just as she was convinced he really was dead, the proprietor of the store came out with several raw chickens in a pail and Albert began to stir. The chickens were wrapped in white butcher's paper, but that didn't stop him from opening his huge jaws and swallowing them whole, paper and all. When feeding time was over, he subsided once more into his motionless state. Amy thought the show was over, but then Albert opened one of his bulbous yellow eyes and stared unblinking at Clara. She looked back at him, seemingly hypnotized by this ancient prisoner in his tiny prison cell. For a long time, they gazed at each other. Kindred spirits in a cruel world.

"Oh, Amy look," Clara sighed. "He wants to go home."

"Someday we'll come back and set him free, Honey. What do you say?"

"I say, 'Hooray." Clara took a loonie from her purse and put it in the donation box beside the fence. Amy wondered what the locals would make of that.

Chapter 10

They were within five miles of the Florida border, the promised land, when Amy noticed the flashing lights in her rear-view mirror. She slowed down and waited for the state trooper to take off after some other unsuspecting traveller in the traffic up ahead. If there was a God, Amy thought, the cop would be chasing that asshole in the black convertible who had passed her like she was standing still and given her a rude hand sign on his way by. But when the patrol car pulled in front of her and slowed down, Amy realized with horror that she was the one who was being stopped. She almost ran into the rear of the cruiser before pulling over to the side of the road. As she waited for what seemed an eternity for the cop to run her licence plate and figure out that they were criminals, Clara dozed beside her, unaware of the impending doom, but Amy knew this was the end of the road.

At last a tall, broad-shouldered young man in uniform sauntered back to stand at her window. Amy saw her life flash before her eyes as she stared into his mirrored sunglasses. She had never been arrested before, but she had watched enough crime shows on tv to know what would happen next. They'd be cuffed and taken back to some dimly lit police station in the last town they had passed, then thrown into a small airtight room with no windows, separated from the rest of humanity by a two-way mirror on the wall. After a long while, an over-weight detective with a shiny bald head and sweat stains under his arms would come in and read them their rights.

He'd try to make Clara crack and say that she had been kidnapped, and God only knows what Clara would do. She sometimes looked at Amy like she'd never seen her before. Amy's imagination moved into overdrive:

"Name?" the guy would say.

"Of course, I have a name. Doesn't everyone?" Clara would give him one of her flirtatious looks and a big smile. She'd always liked a man in uniform.

"I'd advise you not to be too funny, lady. You're in serious trouble here. Now what's your name?

"Don't be rude, young man."

"Sorry. Please tell me your name."

"Clara Johnson." Clara inconveniently remembering her maiden name.

"That's not the name on your health card." He'd move in for the kill.

"Do I have a health card?"

"Yes, I have it right here. It was in your purse."

"Give me that, Fatboy. That's mine! Help, help! This guy stole my purse!"

Oh shit, they'd lock them both up and throw away the key.

By the time the cop opened his pad and took a pen from his pocket, Amy was in a state of shock brought on by her wild imaginings.

"Licence and registration, please Ma'am," the officer said politely.

Amy scrambled in her purse for her licence. Then she reached over Clara's knees to get the ownership from the glove compartment, being careful not to touch her. The cop took a long look at Clara, who was still dead to the world with her mouth open.

9249* by Mary Haylock

"Is she alright?" he asked.

"She's not feeling well. She has the flu."

He drew back from the window a bit. "Do you know why I stopped y'all Ma'am?"

"Yes, I do, Officer. But if you have any heart, you'll let us go." Amy coughed a couple of times out the window trying to sound sick. "You have no idea how long we've been on the road and how far we've come. We just want to go to Florida and spend our last days sitting in the sun. Is that such a crime?" The tears in Amy's eyes were real ones. She couldn't believe that their great adventure had come to this ignominious end when they were so close to their goal. Now she would probably rot in some Georgia jail and Clara would be taken back to wither away among the Daffies at Spring Garden Manor. They would never see each other again. The tears spilled over and ran down Amy's cheeks.

The cop ripped the top paper off his pad and crumpled it in his hand. "Okay, I'll let you off with a warning this time. Get on your way. But try to keep up with the flow of traffic. You know, going thirty miles an hour on a major highway like this one is as bad as speeding. It's slow drivers like you who cause half the accidents. Maybe if you're tired y'all should stop and rest awhile. Y'all have a good day now, y'heah?'" He touched the brim of his hat politely and walked back to his cruiser.

Amy sat perfectly still. She was afraid to move. Somebody up there is looking after us, she thought. Is it you, Gord? Whoever it was, Amy knew they were damned lucky. Clara began to stir, so Amy got up her nerve and sped back into the nearest lane of traffic. Like a baby, Clara was lulled back to sleep by the motion of the car. She missed the whole thing.

9249* by Mary Haylock

Amy had to laugh when she thought about it. She had just got out of a traffic ticket because she was old and pathetic. She remembered a time long ago when Clara had been driving them out for dinner, speeding as usual, when they got pulled over. Clara dodged the bullet by charming the policeman who came onto her and wanted to give her more than a ticket. She had always been such a cute little thing, sort of helpless and feminine, just the kind of woman who made men feel good. Amy was taller and heavier and made men wary with her sarcastic tongue. She envied Clara. Somehow, though, they made a good pair. And now it seemed funny to Amy that she was the one who had talked him out of a ticket, not with her pretty face and figure, like Clara had done, but because she was old and probably reminded the guy of his grandmother.

"If it smells like Florida and it looks like Florida, then it must be Florida." Amy smiled to herself twenty minutes later when they crossed the state line on I-95. She had just caught a breath of the fresh Atlantic breeze coming in the car window and seen the huge oak trees along the sides of the road draped with their customary grey veils of Spanish moss. Clara was still asleep. Amy took the first rest stop she could find and sat in the parking area for a while, trying to pull herself together. It had been such a close call with that cop, and she had been scared for both of them. For the first time Amy wondered what would really happen if they got caught. She was sure that Clara's daughters would never let her near their mother again. And there was no one to talk to about her fears.

She might just as well be alone. After a few minutes Clara woke up and tried to undo her seatbelt. Her eyes had a blank, furtive look.

"Come on, kiddo. We're in Florida! Let's get out and have a stretch. I'm stiff as a board from sitting so long, how about you?"

9249* by Mary Haylock

Clara didn't respond. She got out of the car when Amy undid her seatbelt and started to walk back toward the highway. "Hey, where are you going?" Amy followed her through the parking lot. Clara was walking so fast that Amy had to run to catch up. She grabbed Clara's arm and held on as Clara swung around and took a swipe at Amy with her purse.

"Stop that. Clara, what's wrong with you? Come here. Let's go in for a pee. Come on." Amy dragged a reluctant Clara back toward the rest station and into the washroom.

"Where are we going?" It was a question Amy had heard so often she had begun to hate the sound of it. After all they'd been through Clara was still asking the same thing. And suddenly Amy realized that she probably always would. This whole cockamamie scheme had been Amy's idea. Clara had no idea what was happening. And Amy had a horrible feeling that she wouldn't really care if she did know.

Amy's altruistic motives had gotten her in trouble before. Like the fiasco of the Woodburn General store. When Gord retired early at fifty-two, she had decided he needed something to keep him occupied so she talked him into buying the small general store near their home and becoming a storekeeper. It would be good for him to have a reason to get up out of bed in the morning. The job was endless and didn't make enough of a profit for Gord to hire someone to relieve him. Since Amy was still teaching, he had to do it all himself and instead of enjoying some freedom after working all his life, he was now tied to the little store night and day. He lasted a year. Then they sold the business and broke even.

Undaunted, when Amy retired, she dreamed up the idea of selling their house and buying a cottage on Lake Erie and a mobile home in Florida. Gord would have some fun fixing up both places to suit them, she thought. The snowbird idea turned out better than the store one, although he spent many hours working at both places. Gord seemed happy for those few years before he died, but maybe he would have liked a choice. Why did she always think she was doing people a favour when she insisted on one of her impulsive ideas?

It was the same for Clara. The last few days must have seemed like an endless confusing panorama of strange places and unknown people to her, with Amy as the one faint thread of familiarity running throughout. Maybe what Clara really wanted to say was, 'Why are we going somewhere?' and 'What will happen to me then?' but it always came out the same, 'Where are we going?'

It will be better when we get to a permanent location where we can settle in and Clara can develop a routine, Amy thought. She fervently hoped this would be true but had begun to have doubts. But for now, they just had to keep going. They had come too far to quit. She could almost feel the soft white sand of the beach under her feet and see the blue gulf waters rolling in to meet them, waiting to mend Clara's confused mind and make everything right again. In just a few more hours they would be home.

It took longer than Amy thought to cross the state from east to west on Highway 310, an old two-lane road that meandered through every small town in its path. By the time they reached the Gulf side, it was late, and she had to stop for the night. Gord had prided himself on being able to make the Florida trip in three days, but with all the extra pit stops for Clara, who seemed to like to mark her territory wherever they went, it had taken Amy an extra day. She had thought it best to take their time and take lots of pee breaks, especially since she had been really pushing the water into Clara. Even then there had been a couple of little accidents along the way. When Amy stopped at a drugstore to get a pair of earplugs for Clara, she also bought some Depends and took them with her into the next rest stop:

9249* by Mary Haylock

"Look Clara. I noticed you were running low on underpants, so I bought these for you. Try them on so I can see if they fit. I got pink 'because I know that's your favourite colour."

"They don't fit. They're too big. Why are they so thick?" Clara had pulled them up to her knees and stopped.

"They're nice and puffy so you'll be comfy in them. Like sitting on a pink cloud."

"Bullshit! They're diapers. I know diapers when I see them." Clara pushed them off with her foot and stomped on them."

"But Honey, sometimes we have to drive a long way to the next bathroom, and these will help. Put them on, Clara, please."

"Diapers! I'm not a baby. How could you do that?" she yelled, glaring at Amy. She gave the offending undies a kick that sent them flying under the washroom door. Amy heard a muffled giggle from outside where two teenage girls had been fixing their faces at the mirror.

"Would you mind kicking those back under this door?" Amy wiggled her fingers under the door so they could see.

"Eew," the girls squealed in horrified unison, "Granny pants!" They pushed open the door to the washroom and bolted out. Amy gave up and made sure Clara wore dark slacks and sat on the car rug when they were driving. In the mid-day heat of Florida, the car started to smell bad and so did Clara. Amy tried to get her into the shower at the motel that night, but Clara refused, and Amy couldn't budge her. Finally, she stopped trying, sprayed Clara with her lily-of-the-valley cologne and fell into bed exhausted from the long day.

9249* by Mary Haylock

There were no bad dreams, no apparitions by the bed trying to snuff her out. Just a long peaceful night of 'down the well' sleep for Amy. But when she woke up Clara was gone – again.

Chapter 11

The motel was in horse country on the outskirts of a little ranch community just before the road reached I-75. Amy searched the grounds after checking in the lobby to see if Clara was having coffee and the free muffin advertised on the sign outside the office. The clerk on duty said she'd been there all morning and hadn't seen anyone come in. Amy began to feel sick. She came to a board fence on the north side of the motel property and scanned the fields beyond. Several times she saw a moving shape in the distance, but when she squinted hard into her sunglasses, she could see that it was a horse grazing in the sunshine. They were dotted about the field standing alone or in small groups, swishing their tails and cropping the sparse grass. Amy felt a faint hope rising in her chest.

Clara loved horses. In fact, Clara loved anything with four legs; cats, dogs, squirrels, rabbits, even donkeys. In Greece after they had paid several euros for a donkey ride up to a temple on a hill in Lindos, Clara refused to get on because she said her donkey was too small for such a heavy load. She led him gently up to the top much to the consternation of the donkey's owner, who followed her yelling loudly in Greek. When he took his stick and smacked Amy's donkey on the rear to keep him going, Clara grabbed the stick and broke it in half over her knee. The exasperated donkey man had taken both animals back down the hill and left Clara and Amy to walk down on their own. If there were animals in that field, chances are Clara would be there too.

Amy climbed the three rails of the fence and clung precariously to the top rail. Her sciatica made her wince with pain, but she didn't stop trying until she managed to throw her leg over and make her way back down the other side. She looked for any signs that Clara had been there but saw nothing but a few piles of horse manure here and there. Stepping carefully, she made her way to the crest of a hill where she hoped to be able to see to the other side. God, let Clara be there, she prayed. When she reached the top, winded and aching all over from the effort, she saw only more fields and more horses. Several of them raised their heads at the sight of Amy and started to follow her at a distance, curious, no doubt, about this intruder. Amy hoped they were mares or geldings. The stallion might not find her encroachment so amusing.

Far off to the left, the open field rolled downhill into a swale surrounded by trees and bushes. There'd be water there, Amy thought. And this was Florida. There'd be 'gators there too! Amy started to run, panting for breath and calling as loudly as she could, "Clara, Clara!" The horses whinnied and wheeled around heading for the far side of the pasture. This strange creature looked dangerous to them Amy could picture Clara walking right up to an alligator and trying to pat it. She ran faster than her sciatica usually allowed without once feeling the pain of it. At the bottom of the hill a swampy area led to a little pond surrounded by willows.

At the edge of the pond, with her shoes and socks off and her feet dangling in the murky brown water sat Clara. She took no notice when Amy came puffing up behind her, just swished her toes back and forth making little ripples in the water, a tempting bait for 'gators or snapping turtles.

With the little bit of strength, she had left Amy hurled herself at Clara and pulled her away from the edge of the pond. They ended up in a tangled heap on the grass:

9249* by Mary Haylock

"Clara, get away from there. There might be 'gators in that water."

"Don't be silly. There's nothing in here but goldfish. Fred likes to sit on the edge and look at them, but he can't catch them. He doesn't like to get his feet wet." Clara laughed remembering her cat's aversion to water. "Come on, put your feet in Scaredy Cat."

Amy dried Clara's feet with the tail of her shirt, put on her shoes and socks and pulled her up by both hands. Clara took off up the hill, jogging easily along. Amy started after her but stiffened up halfway and had to stop.

"Clara, wait up. Wait for me!" Amy was wheezing now. She could hardly breathe. Up ahead she heard Clara laughing as she skipped along the top of the hill and then disappeared over the other side.

"Clara, Clara. Come back!" Amy was desperate now. She didn't want to lose her again. "Look, Clara. I found a baby rabbit. Come and see it." She cupped her hands around an imaginary bunny and held her breath until Clara's head came back into view.

"Let me see it. Is it alright?" Clara started back down the hill toward Amy. When she got close enough Amy grabbed her arm and held on tight.

"Where's Fred?" Clara asked in a plaintive tone. "I can't find him."

"He's gone fishing. Come on."

"Where are we going?"

9249* by Mary Haylock

Amy started to cry, big racking sobs that came out between wheezes. Clara seemed not to notice. When Amy could talk again, she turned Clara around and looked her right in the eye. "We're going to a place where we'll be free. We can swim every day and play in the surf like we used to do and lie in the sun and eat fried shrimp the size of basketballs in a little restaurant on the beach under a palm tree."

"Sounds like Heaven," Clara said. "Let's go!"

Back on the road again they finally made the turn onto I-75, the last leg of their journey, Amy started to get excited. They were almost there. Another four hours on the road and they'd be in Punta Gorda. The rolling hills of north Florida gradually gave way to level land and the highway stretched out long and shimmering in the noonday heat. She had lots of time to think since Clara was once again asleep beside her.

What was it about this terrible disease of hers that made Clara feel empathy for a strange animal and nothing for her companion's obvious distress, Amy wondered. Why was she so territorial about her things and her money now, when she had always been the most generous of friends? How could she sing every song she'd ever heard and remember the story of how she was born but couldn't remember where she was going or carry on a meaningful conversation about something in the here and now? Milton got it right when he said, *"The mind is its own place and makes a Heaven of Hell, a Hell of Heaven."* He must have known someone with Alzheimer's, Amy thought.

She wondered what was happening at home. Surely by now they would have figured out what happened to Clara. Her daughters would get in touch with Amy's boys and they'd be able to guess where they were headed. Why didn't the cops come looking for them? Amy had a sudden horrible thought. Maybe the kids didn't really care. Now they were gone, they didn't have to worry about their crazy mothers anymore. She could just imagine the talk:

Hi, Tom? Tom Winston? . . . It's Debbie Cunningham, remember me? . . . I know. Listen Tom, our mom has escaped from the nursing home. and we think maybe your mom is with her. She's been gone for four days now . . . Have you seen your mom lately? . . .

Oh, to Ottawa eh. Do you think she was telling the truth?. . . Because she was seen with mom on the day she disappeared. . .Well that might explain why you can't get hold of her. . . .Can you imagine those two crazy old ladies?. . . .Where do you think they might have gone? . . .

We've notified the police and they've searched the area near the home but couldn't find any sign of her. . . . . .I know, it would be just like your mom to do it. She didn't like it when we put mom in there, but we had to, you know. She just couldn't look after herself anymore.

So Tom, if you could give us your mom's licence number the police could look for her car. I hope they're together. . .At least your mom has a few marbles left. . .

You might think of putting her in a safe place when we find them, though. They're both getting kinda weird.. . .

Okay, thanks. I'll keep in touch.

Soon the net would be cast and given the state of international communications nowadays it wouldn't be long until they were caught. Amy knew they had to get where they were going and get off the highway as soon as possible. Then they could lie low in some little backwater trailer park until Clara was better.

She tramped on the gas pedal and tried to get up to the speed limit and stay there. The PT had cruise control, but Amy had never used it. She didn't like the out-of-control feeling of flying along at the same speed all the time, no matter what was happening up ahead. She liked to feel that imperceptible adjustment of the driver's foot on the gas to show he was aware of the traffic conditions. It gave her a sense of being in control, even when she wasn't driving. Gord had liked to use the cruise on long stretches of highway because it let him stretch his right leg a bit, but he usually didn't bother because he knew Amy wasn't happy when he did. Just another one of the ways he accommodated her wishes in spite of his own discomfort. God, she felt sorry for him for having put up with her all those years.

Why is it that we think we're just great all our lives and then when we get old, we can clearly see the chinks in our own armour? Why do we have to wait until it's almost too late before we finally see the truth about ourselves. Is it so we have time to make some much needed amends before we head for the great beyond? Amy wished she was Catholic. Her confessional might go like this:

"Bless me father for I have sinned. It's been seventy years since my last confession."
"I gather you're not Catholic. But what the hell, I have a few hours to spare, so tell me about it."
"Well, I always think I'm right and I try to make other people do what I think they should and sometimes it's not so great for them."
"Can you give me an example?"
"I drove my husband nuts by always thinking up things for him to do when all he ever wanted was to play golf with his friend Leonard."
"Ah golf, a sin for sure. And what else, my child?"
"I tell my grandchildren what subjects they should take in school and how they should choose a good profession that makes a lot of money when they just want to do their own thing."
"This is not such a crime. Kids need a push nowadays. What else?"

9249* by Mary Haylock

"This is the worst one, Father. I kidnapped my friend Clara from the home where her children had put her to keep her safe and she is all confused and unhappy. I thought I was doing her a favour, but now I'm not so sure."

"Okay, tell you what. God will forgive you and take you into Heaven if you convert. It will just take a minute. We call it a 'deathbed conversion'."

"Am I going to die?"

"Of course, why do you think they called me? I was out on the golf course with the bishop. Two under par. Now let's get at it."

"What if I don't convert, what will become of me then?"

"My dear child, you have always had the power to go to Heaven. Just hang onto my crucifix and click your heels together three times and say, 'I am not agnostic, I am not agnostic, I am not agnostic'...."

Amy came out of her daydream when Clara woke up in an agitated state. She thrashed around in her seat pulling on the seatbelt that held her firmly in place. Amy tried to make out what she was saying, but after while realized it made no sense at all.

"I can't find him. No, no. Where is he?" she babbled.

"Clara, Honey, it's okay. Look out the window. We're almost there. You can see Tampa Bay out the window. And way out there is the Gulf of Mexico. Look, Clara."

"No! Don't tamper with it. Go away. I don't want a haircut. Leave me alone. No, no!"

"Please, Clara. Be quiet! Look at the water. See the big bridge that goes to St. Petersburg? You and I have been on that bridge before. Remember?" Amy was having trouble keeping her mind on her driving with all the commotion in the car.

"St. Peter is at the pearly gates. Let me out! I don't want to go in there! Clara was rubbing her hands raw from scraping them on the seatbelt. There was no where to pull over. Amy looked around in desperation and found a Cd. in the pocket of the door on her side of the car. She opened it and inserted it in the slot on the dash. It was Willie Nelson with his familiar comforting twang singing, *Blue Eyes Cryin' in the Rain.*

Clara settled back in her seat and joined Willie in perfect unison. She turned her head and smiled at Amy who breathed a sigh of relief. Thank God for music and for Willie.

Chapter 12

Amy took highway 17 west off I-75 following the signs to Fisherman's Wharf, the big tourist attraction in Punta Gorda. They were here at last. Several trailer parks along the way advertised places for rent but Amy didn't like the looks of them. She remembered one that was right on the Peace River. It was old but most of the units had stood their ground through fifty years of hurricanes and tornados. Some had little gardens and porches added on recently and pots of flowers hanging in the lanai.

Tropical Gardens, the sign at the road announced proudly, having lost its r in some big wind long ago. Amy pulled in and surveyed the place. What looked suspiciously like an old army barracks had a sign over the door that said, Clubhouse. Beside it was a rectangular pool surrounded by cement and enclosed by a wire fence. A few white plastic lawn chairs were scattered around the edge. No one was in the water. Near the gate a crumbling statue of a dolphin arched over the opening. A small building on the other side of the pool advertised itself as *The Office*. It supported a huge, magenta bougainvillea in full bloom beside the doorway.

Amy got out and stretched her legs before she went around to undo Clara's seatbelt. She didn't wake up, so Amy went inside leaving Clara asleep in the car. While she waited for someone to show up Amy read the ads on the wall showing several trailers that were for rent. There were a few that looked quite nice and Amy was hopeful that she could find something suitable for the two of them. The prices didn't seem too bad and right now the loonie was holding its own with the dollar, so that was good.

In a few minutes, a golf cart pulled up in front and a man with a deep tan and a lined face got out and came in. He greeted Amy and showed her the pictures of the trailers that were still for rent. It was off season now, he said, so the prices had come down. She was a lucky little lady.

Amy had just about made up her mind which ones she wanted to look at, when she heard another car pull into the parking lot. When she turned to look out the window, it wasn't another car, it was her car. She watched in horror as the PT swung around in the driveway, kicking up a cloud of dust and narrowly missing the playful dolphin. Then it took off lurching and swaying down one of the little streets of the park at a great speed. Amy remembered that she had left the keys in the ignition. Someone had stolen her car. And then she got a good look at the person driving. With a fiendish expression on her face and her elbow jauntily protruding from the window it was Clara at the wheel!

"We've got to catch her. Help me. She doesn't know what she's doing!" Amy ran out the door and started to run after the car.

"Come on, get in." yelled the man as he jumped into the golf cart. They took off after Clara as fast as they could go. It wasn't fast enough. Clara wove back and forth through the streets of the little trailer park, just missing a man walking his dog and a woman in a wheelchair. Amy could hear Clara laughing at these near misses. She stopped a few times, but as soon as they got close to her, she would take off, spinning her wheels and covering the front of the golf cart with dust and gravel. At last she reached the end of the road, where it branched off in two different directions. One way headed to the riverbank where an old rowboat was tied up at a makeshift dock, the other led to a maintenance shed. Clara chose that way. The doors to the shed were open and Clara drove right in. Amy's car disappeared and the engine died. There was silence in the early evening stillness of the Florida countryside. Carefully, Amy and the manager peered into the dark interior of the little building. Somehow, Clara had managed to avoid a riding mower and several cans of gasoline sitting nearby. She was still at the wheel, but not moving at all. Amy ran to the car and looked in the open window, dreading what she might find. Clara turned to smile at her. Her cheeks were pink from the excitement of it all and her eyes were alive and shining.

"Wheeeeee," Clara said.

Amy tried to speak but nothing came out. Then the manager spoke out exasperatedly, ""You're a dang fool, woman. Get out of that shed. And you can both get out of here. There's nothing here for you to rent. Crazy old broads. Hit the road." He climbed back into his cart and took off, stopping on his way to placate the indignant residents who had found themselves in Clara's path.

Amy took Clara by the hand and put her back on her own side of the car, firmly belting her in and making a mental note never to leave her loose in the car again. Then she backed out carefully and headed back to the entrance. She'd have to take her chances at one of the other trailer parks they'd passed on the way here.

Just before they got back to I-75 she found a group of fishing shacks near a boat ramp that led into the Peace River. It would be noisy with the highway so close overhead and the trailers looked really old and in bad shape, but it was dark now, and she'd had about enough of this day.

Once they signed in at the Peace River Fish Camp and grabbed a sandwich at a nearby 7-11, Amy got them both ready for bed. Clara didn't take long to fall asleep after her exciting adventure and Amy made sure she locked the door and kept the key under her pillow. But even though she was bone weary she couldn't fall asleep right away. She had lost Clara twice in one day and both times could have had disastrous results. She could have been bitten by an alligator in the pond at the horse farm or driven off the road into the river in T-opical Gardens, or worse, she could have killed someone.

Amy knew she had to take better care of Clara, had to think ahead and plan what to do with her when she had to leave her alone. It was like having a baby to look after 24-7 with no breaks and no time to let down her guard.

She went to the bathroom and splashed cool water on her face. As she pulled the towel away and peered into the mirror, she could see she had aged about ten years on this trip. Her eyes were in shadow with blue circles underscoring the wrinkled skin around them. Between her brows a semi-permanent little furrow had planted itself and her lips which usually turned up at the corners in a perpetual smile had acquired similar little furrows to match the one in her forehead above.

Her rosacea had flared up already from the short time she'd been in the sun making a red splotch across her nose and down her cheeks. All in all she looked pretty haggard. And no wonder. She hadn't slept well for three nights and she was in constant pain from her arthritis which was crippling her hips and shoulders from long hours of sitting in the car. Clara would owe her a facelift and a Swedish massage when they got settled in.

Amy tried to maintain her positive attitude, but she was really beginning to understand why Clara's girls had to put her in Spring Garden Manor. With husbands and jobs and kids of their own they couldn't give her the constant supervision and care that

9249* by Mary Haylock

she needed. Amy didn't want to admit it, but she was beginning to doubt that she could do it either.

She turned out the light and tip-toed over to the bed to look down at Clara who looked younger and more alive than she had for ages. Her skin was beginning to turn that warm brown from the sun that always made Amy had been jealous of how easily the sun turned Clara's skin golden when they were young.

Amy, with her Irish ancestry, looked more like a boiled lobster. But Clara was the picture of glowing good health. It was enough to make Amy want to keep trying. Once they'd recovered from the trip, they could start having some fun.

She decided to take Clara to Fisherman's Wharf for dinner tomorrow. Maybe she'd start remembering some of the good times they'd had there, sitting out on the porch at the river's edge watching the pelicans dive for their dinner, drinking margaritas and eating mussels from a steam pot, waiting for the sun to go down in one of those spectacular sunset displays Florida is famous for, all orange and red and yellow. That might be just what Clara needed to get her memory back in working order again. It was a long shot, but worth the try.

"Amy." It was hardly more than a whisper from the dim shape on the bed, but it made Amy's heart stop beating for a second.

"What is it, Honey?
"I had a great time today. Thank you."

Tears stung Amy's eyes. It was the first time since they left home that Clara had said her name.

The earplugs really helped with Clara's sleeping and this in turn gave Amy a more restful night. She woke the next day to brilliant sunshine and a feeling of great accomplishment. She'd done it. She'd rescued Clara from that awful place and here they were in Florida, free at last.

Their little cabin was right next to the boat ramp and already there were several trailers lined up to launch their boats in the river. Groups of men stood around telling lies and fiddling with their fishing gear as they waited their turn. Clara smiled and waved at several of them as she and Amy got into their car to go shopping at Publix in town. Amy decided it would be fun, and also cheaper to eat at home most of the time, so they were off to buy some groceries. There was a rickety wooden picnic table outside their door and beside it a rusty barbecue but the guy who signed them in said it worked and still had lots of gas from the last tenants. There was a small fridge in the kitchen of the cabin and after she cleaned out the styrofoam container of old bait and plugged it in Amy could tell that it was working okay. She made a list of the things they needed and took note of the charges on her credit card.

So far, the trip had cost over eight hundred dollars, but most of that was for gas and eating out. It wouldn't be so expensive now they were settled in one place. Best of all, no one would ever think to look for them here. The cabin was surrounded by a hedge of mangroves making the car invisible from the road. It was the perfect hideaway for two old babes on the run.

As they approached town, the traffic seemed much heavier than Amy remembered. People were parked all over the edge of the public park and crowds had gathered there near the pavilion, where the local high school band was playing something that vaguely resembled a Sousa march. Beyond the park, the road was blocked by barricades and a police car with its lights blinking. Amy took the first spot at the side of the road that she could find, and she and Clara went hand in hand to see what was happening. A sign in front of the band stand said, 'Memorial Day Concert, May

9249* by Mary Haylock

19th'. Amy remembered this was always quite a celebration here, sort of like Victoria Day at home in Canada.

Amy wondered what they were doing back there. A long time ago when she and Gord lived at the lake they always had a barbecue with the kids and grandkids complete with sparklers and fireworks. Lately, though, the boys hadn't bothered with that stuff. The kids were all grown up now and too sophisticated to wave a sparkler around and try to spell their names in the air.

Clara was enjoying the crowd and the excitement. She marched in place in time to the music, raising her knees high and swinging her free arm back and forth.

"Come on, let's go," Clara shouted above the noise. Amy kept tight hold of her other arm in case Clara decided to march off into the river. When the band finished playing Clara clapped long and loudly.

"Bravo, bravo!" she yelled. The conductor looked over his shoulder and smiled at her.

"Okay, that's enough clapping," Amy said. "They weren't that good." She pulled Clara away from the bandstand and they walked the rest of the way to the grocery store down the street. It was just as Amy remembered it. At the doorway, an older man greeted them and gave them a cart to use. Clara thanked him profusely, still on a high from the band music. Then they started down the first aisle to find what was on the list. It was like shopping with a child. Clara wanted everything; a bottle of wine, olive oil in a huge tin, grits, cheese and crackers of every description, and even condoms in a large economy size box that promised 'ecstasy for her!'

"You think you're going to get lucky, old gal?" Amy laughed as she put the box back on the shelf.

9249* by Mary Haylock

In the produce department Clara stood fascinated by the mist of water that freshened the vegetables every few minutes. She put out her hands and closed her eyes, laughing each time the cool water surprised her fingers.

"Look. Niagara Falls!" Clara said.

Finally, Amy got Clara moving by letting her push the cart. This had the added benefit of making it harder for Clara to grab things off the shelves. By the time they reached the checkout, Amy was exhausted, Clara was munching on a banana and the buggy was filled with many little surprises. They had spent twice as much as Amy estimated but Clara was happy and taking an active part in the whole adventure. To Amy that was worth the few extra dollars.

When they got back to the cabin, they put the groceries away in the two little cupboards above the sink and Amy made them a glass of lemonade. There were two wooden chairs out front by the river, where the mangroves had been chopped down and Clara and Amy sat there looking out on the wide expanse of the Peace River.

Little boats bobbed up and down in the current and a large shrimper headed for shore with his morning catch weighing the boat down almost to the gunwales. Amy made a mental note to go to the dock in town and get some shrimp fresh off the boat for supper some night. But for tonight she wanted to go to Fisherman's Wharf. Maybe Clara would start remembering there.

After lunch, Amy couldn't wait to go to the beach. She packed up their beach stuff, got both of them into their bathing suits and headed for the Gulf. It was a 'high blue' day with the sun beating down but not too much humidity, a perfect day to be out in the sun. Amy headed for Manasota Key, her favourite spot for lolling on the white gulf sands..

9249* by Mary Haylock

They were lucky and found a parking space not too far away and in no time, Amy had set up the umbrella and the beach towels. She was surprised at how empty the beach was, until she remembered that they were in the off season, not at the high time when they used to be here. The tourists would have headed home at the end of April.

Clara allowed Amy to slather her with sunscreen and then she propped her head on some towels and started to look at the book Amy handed her. It was one she had brought from the home; the same one Clara had been reading since she got there. It was about cats.

"What're you reading?" Amy asked.

"A book."

"What's it about?"

"I don't know."

"Isn't it about cats? It says so on the front."

Clara turned the book over and looked at the front cover. "I guess so."

"What does it say?" Amy began to wonder if Clara could still read.

"I don't know."

"You've been reading that same page for half an hour. What does it say?"

"It says you're full of shit!" Clara slammed the book shut and closed her eyes. She didn't like questions. They spent the next few hours in silence, listening to the waves lapping on the shore.

Amy was almost asleep when she felt Clara get up and head toward the water.

"Where are you going?"

"Swimming."

"Okay, wait for me." Amy had bought a couple of styro-foam belts to keep them afloat. She wasn't sure that Clara would remember how to swim. Before she could put the flotation device on her, Clara ran into the surf and dove in headfirst. Amy held her breath until she saw Clara's curly head pop up on the other side of the wave. She waved at Amy who was trying to do up her belt.

Then Clara turned and headed full steam out to sea. She had always been a good swimmer, and apparently, she hadn't forgotten how. Amy's heart sank as she watched Clara taking her familiar crisp little overhand strokes and moving quickly through the water. She was well beyond Amy's reach now, on her way to Mexico.

"Clara," Amy called as loudly as she could. "Come back." To her surprise, Clara stopped swimming and turned over on her back. She floated back toward shore on the next wave, ending up right beside Amy.

"Come on, slowpoke. Surf's up!" Clara was having a great time.

When Amy got out of the water after an hour of splashing around, her fingers were pruney and she was tired. Clara didn't want to get out. Amy watched her riding the waves for a while and then came to the water's edge and captured her hand, leading her back to the towels. They lay down and dozed in the heat until their suits were dry and then Amy packed up and took Clara back to the car.

When they got home it was time to shower off the salty residue of the gulf water and get dressed for dinner. Clara was really turning brown now from their day in the sun. Amy dressed her up in a blue sundress that matched the colour of her eyes. She looked healthy and as pretty as Amy had seen her look for ages. Amy, on the other hand, was red all over. The hot Florida sun had burned right through her SPF 60 tanning lotion. She felt hot and scratchy in whatever she put on, so finally she settled for a long sundress with small straps. The less material she had touching her skin the better.

Amy remembered the way to Fisherman's Wharf, and she found a parking spot easily near the entrance to the long wooden pier that jutted out into the Peace River. Much of it was built on a spit of land with shops on either side selling tourist clothing and gifts. The main restaurant was at the end, built right out over the water on wooden piers. When they arrived, they were lucky to get a table at the edge where they could watch the seagulls and pelicans swooping down for their dinner in the copper- coloured water.

Clara seemed fascinated by the antics of the gulls, who brazenly passed closely overhead in hopes of a tidbit or two being tossed their way. When the waiter brought some rolls in a basket Clara threw a whole one at a low flying bird who followed it right down into the water and came up triumphant, with the soggy prize in its beak. Amy restrained her when she reached for another and the food arrived before Clara could argue about it.

Amy had ordered a grouper sandwich for each of them and it was served with fries in a small basket lined with a checkered napkin. Amy doctored up the fries with salt and vinegar the way Clara liked them and took some of the onion off the bun. Then she fixed her own dinner and took a bite of the sandwich. It tasted great, just the way she remembered it from long ago.

Clara picked up a fry and took a dainty bite from one end of it before another cheeky gull swooped down on her and she pitched the rest at him. He caught it in mid-air and settled himself on a post nearby to gobble it down. Clara grabbed a handful of fries and threw them at him, causing him to set up a great squawking and flapping of wings. Several other gulls landed nearby to try to get in on the bonanza. They came to rest on a sign near the fence that said, 'Please don't feed the birds."

"Excuse me, Miss." The waiter addressed himself to Clara. "We ask that customers don't feed the gulls. They get really aggressive if you do." He smiled a tight little smile and turned to go.

"Screw you!" Clara said. She took another handful of fries and threw them at his departing back.

"Hey, lady, knock it off! What's the matter with you?" He came back to the table and glared down at Clara, hands on his hips. "If you try that again you're out of here!"

Amy half rose from her chair and tried to get his attention. When he looked at her, she made a circling motion around her ear until he finally got the message.

"Sorry Miss," he said. Then he looked at Clara and spoke in a loud voice. "You enjoy your dinner, now. Okay, Lady?" He picked up the fries and scurried back to the kitchen.

Clara put her hands in her lap and looked out over the water.

"Eat your grouper, Clara. It's really good. Remember how you like fish?" Amy coaxed.

9249* by Mary Haylock

"Fred likes fish. Where's Fred?" Clara looked around with a puzzled expression.

"Fred's at home, Honey."

"I'll take this home for him." Clara wrapped the burger up in the napkin and put it in her purse while Amy took a few more bites of her own dinner. Then they left the restaurant. It didn't seem to be a good night for remembering after all.

Chapter 13

"Did you have fun today?" Amy asked. They were ready for bed when she decided to test Clara's memory of the day's events. She knew that it was short term memory that was most affected by Alzheimer's and she wanted a kind of benchmark for future reference so she could see if Clara was getting better now she was out in the world instead of being locked in the repressive atmosphere of the Daffy ward.

"Yes." Clara pulled back the covers and started to lie down on her bed.

"What did you like best?"

"Best about what?"

"Best about all the fun things we did today."

"What fun things did we do?" Clara looked genuinely puzzled by Amy's question.

"Don't you remember anything we did?"

"Of course, I do."

"Well, what did you like best?" Amy fought to keep her voice steady and calm.

"I liked the cows." Clara smiled at Amy hopefully.

"What cows? We didn't see any cows."

"I did."

"Where did you see cows?"

"What cows?"

"The cows you said you saw."

"Did I see cows?"

Amy crawled into bed and pulled the covers over her head. She stuffed the pillow into her mouth and screamed at the top of her voice. Then she got out of bed, handed Clara her earplugs and tucked the covers around her.

"Good-night, Sweetie. Sleep tight."

"Don't let the bedbugs bite," Clara called back smiling up at Amy, who leaned over and gave her a kiss on the cheek.

That night Amy dreamed of cows. They had long curved horns like the ones she'd seen that day over the door of the Longhorn Café when they stopped for lunch. She was chasing a bunch of them along a beach. For some reason she knew she had to catch them and put them back in their pen before something disastrous happened, but she couldn't keep up.

A flock of seagulls was following the herd, flying just above their heads and swooping down on them every once in a while. Then she saw Clara riding on the lead cow, laughing and waving at Amy as she urged the animal to go faster and faster until they were out of sight.

9249* by Mary Haylock

When Amy woke up, she was soaked in sweat and breathing hard. It took a long time to get back to sleep and when she finally did, she slept fitfully. In the morning she woke up tired and depressed. Her shoulders and hips hurt from all that frolicking about in the surf and she was pink and itchy from the sun that had burned its way through her lotion. Worst of all, Clara remembered nothing.

Amy tried again to help her recall what they'd done the day before, but she still drew a blank.

"Remember the waves at the beach, Clara?" Amy asked.

"Sure, it was fun." Clara wanted to please her, but Amy knew she didn't have a clue about where they'd been. What was the use of trying to fill Clara's days with exciting things to do when they disappeared from her memory almost immediately? No wonder people gave up on their loved ones and left them alone. There was no reward in it at all. Except that during the time it was happening, Clara had been having a wonderful time. Amy knew from the smile on her face and the light in her eyes. Did it really matter that she couldn't bring it back to mind later? Maybe not.

"We sure had lots of fun. We played in the water, in those nice big waves and then we sat in the sun on our beach towels just like we used to when we were young. And then we had a freezie at that little store across from the beach. What a great day!"

While Amy talked, Clara listened with her whole body. It was like going to the beach again for her. Amy would have to do the remembering for both of them. They didn't have to do something special every day. Amy just had to tell Clara they did. It was good just to relax and sit in the chairs out front and look at the water. Maybe they'd get some of that shrimp for dinner tonight, Amy thought. She needed a day to rest up. Looking after Clara was like having a full-time job.

Amy got to the dock just in time to get one of the last bags of shrimp. They were nice big ones and she thought she might deep fry them in the little fryer she had found at the cabin. It was a good thing that Clara had put that big tin of oil in the buggy in the supermarket. Now all she needed was some Aunt Jemima pancake mix. That's how Gord had cooked them. He just made a thin pancake mixture with water and dipped the shrimp in, then dunked them in the sizzling oil for a few minutes. Amy was sure she could do that too. She remembered how good they'd tasted. And now it didn't matter how fattening they were since neither she nor Clara cared anymore. At seventy-five there were damn few pleasures left in life, and eating was one of them. So, what if they'd live twelve days longer if they gave up saturated fat.

After she and Clara brought home the pancake mix from the Seven-eleven on the highway, Amy remembered at the last minute that the shrimp needed a lemon. It just wouldn't taste right without a lemon. Looking out the window over the sink she saw a small lemon tree down by the river. Most of the fruit had fallen off, but a few remained clinging stubbornly to the branches.

Taking Clara by the hand she went out to pick some. They might still be edible, although the season for lemons was long past. Amy brought them in and scrubbed the skins until they became yellow instead of black. Then she cut one open to see how it looked inside. Clara looked over her shoulder anxiously.

"Look, Clara, it's okay. Now we have a lemon for our shrimp."

Clara started to sing in a voice reminiscent of Harry Belafonte a song about a Lemon Tree. She danced around the room as she sang, tossing one of the lemons into the air and catching it again. Then she tossed it at Amy, who caught it with one hand and sent it right back to Clara. They played catch for several minutes, laughing at each other when they missed, and only stopping when the lemon began to get soggy on the outside from being dropped on the floor. Amy sat down heavily in one of the wooden kitchen chairs, but Clara didn't want to stop. She continued to throw the lifeless lemon at Amy, hitting her on the face and making a wet mess on the front of her t-shirt.

"Stop it, Clara. That hurt,"

Clara drew back and fired at Amy again, narrowly missing her glasses and leaving a trail of pits across her face. The laughter had gone out of Clara and she looked angry and wild.

"Clara, stop it!" Amy used her sternest schoolteacher voice and Clara subsided into a chair with her head on her chest. "You hurt me, Clara. And look at this poor lemon. We can't eat this one now."

"Blah, blah, blah, blah, blah," Clara mumbled into the front of her shirt.

"Come on," Amy said wearily. "Let's have our shrimp now. They must be cooked to death." She lifted them out of the boiling oil and put them on a paper towel. Then she cut another lemon and put the wedges on a plate for each of them, along with six of the large shrimps. They actually looked pretty good, and after all, the game of lemon toss hadn't done any real harm.

Clara refused to look up or to touch the food on her plate. She just kept on singing:

"Blah, blah black sheep, Have you any wool? Yes sir, yes sir, three bags full"

9249* by Mary Haylock

The shrimp were actually delicious. Amy ate two, but then she couldn't eat any more. It was no good. She'd lost her appetite looking at Clara and listening to her meaningless babble. Amy didn't know how much more she could take. After she cleaned up the mess from dinner, she turned on the small tv set and found 'Jeopardy' on one of the few channels they could get. Clara sat staring, apparently mesmerized by what was on the screen but Amy let her mind wander;

"I'll take Diseases of the Mind for one hundred, Alex."

"A type of dementia characterized by gradual loss of memory."

"What is Alzheimer's?"

"Well done, Amy."

"Diseases of the Mind for two hundred, Alex."

"The prognosis for those who have Alzheimer's."

"What is Death? Alex."

"Good for you, Amy. You are now in the lead with ten thousand dollars. Choose again."

"Diseases of the Mind for three hundred, Alex."

"Zilch."

"What is the likelihood that I can cure my friend of Alzheimer's?"

"Right you are Amy. You are doing very well in this category. Choose again."

"Diseases of the Mind for four hundred, Alex."

"Oh! It's the Daily Double. Good for you Amy. The answer is, 'Zero'."

Tick, tock, tick, tock "Time's up. Let's see what our contestants wrote:

"Fred? You wrote, 'What is the likelihood that I died of old age?' No, I'm sorry Fred."

"Amy? You wrote, 'What are the chances that I will be able to stand another day with Clara?'

9249* by Mary Haylock

"No, I'm sorry Amy, you lose all your money. You are now down to nothing. That makes you the big loser."
"Thankyou Alex.

The next few days were uneventful, and Amy took the opportunity to do some washing at the office, where a couple of ancient machines charged fifty cents a load for the washer and twenty-five for the dryer. The prices hadn't been changed since the Korean war, and that was great, but the machines were also from the same era and made a terrible racket as the clothes plunged around wildly. It took four goes to dry them properly. Clara was quiet and subdued. She sat with Amy on a bench and watched the dryer with the same intense interest that she had shown watching tv. She answered Amy's questions with one word and all attempts at making conversation were futile, so they spent the day without talking.

Amy missed having someone to talk to. She didn't see too much of her boys and their families at home, but they often called to see how she was and once in a while dropped in or took her out for dinner or for a ride. It was a special occasion when the grandchildren came too.

Amy wondered what was happening at home. She longed to hear the sound of their voices, to hear their day to day little adventures, to know they were healthy and safe. She wondered about calling them but thought better of it. They would be able to trace the call and find out where they were. She wasn't about to give up on Clara just yet. She could see little positive signs that made her want to keep on trying. But it sure was lonesome when Clara was in one of her moods. It was like living with a cardboard caricature of her old friend. She was there, but not really there at all. Amy wondered how long this would last. She hoped Clara would come back to her soon.

Chapter 14

After three days of Clara's zombie like state, Amy was going stir-crazy. She decided to go somewhere, anywhere just to have contact with another human being, one who would look at her and speak to her. She was beginning to feel invisible. It was time for an adventure.

Amy had noticed Clara watching the fishermen as they launched their boats at the nearby ramp. She would look up from her book when she heard the motor start up and follow the boat with her eyes until it disappeared down the river. Maybe she would like to go fishing, Amy thought. She talked to the manager of the fish camp and arranged to rent a boat and some gear for the next day.

Then she made a list and headed out for Publix again. This time Clara walked passively beside the cart, hanging onto one side of the handle, and didn't take anything off the shelves or even want to play in the produce spray. It was a much easier shopping expedition than last time, but Amy wished that Clara would show a bit of interest.

"Do you want sandwiches for our picnic tomorrow?" Amy asked when they got to the deli counter.

"Fred likes tuna." Clara's voice was flat.

"Fred's not coming. How about you, what do you want."

"Where are we going?"

"Fishing. We'll have a picnic out on the river. It'll be fun, don't you think?"

"Well, I'm not going."

"Why not? You like to fish."

"How will we get there?"

"In a boat. I rented a little boat for us."

"I can't go."

"Why not?"

"I can't swim."

"Yes, you can."

"Can what?"

"Swim!"

"Where?"

"Never mind, let's get some ham."

As much as she was used to these nowhere conversations with Clara, Amy could still feel the anger rising in her chest. Anger for the insane hope that things would somehow be the way they used to be. *Why do I bother, why?* she asked herself for the umpteenth time.

9249* by Mary Haylock

Back at the cabin Amy cooked some hotdogs for supper on the rusty barbecue while Clara sat in a lawn chair with her book in her lap, pretending to read. Amy could see it was the same page she had been reading for the whole trip. The bookmark had found its eternal resting place on page one hundred and twenty. Amy wondered how Clara had made it that far. Had she really read it at one time and had she stuck the marker there to mark in perpetuity the place where her brain had ceased to function? The sight of Clara in her chair reading a book gave a surreal sense of normalcy to the scene.

There was Clara caught in a moment in time, perpetually observing the printed words on the same page and retaining none of the meaning. It was enough to drive Amy mad.

She doctored up the hotdogs and placed one on a turned over box that acted as a table next to Clara's chair. Clara looked up at Amy and smiled;

"No thank you," she said politely.

"You're welcome," Amy made an exaggerated curtsey. Clara picked up the hotdog and took a dainty bite from the end.

Now I know how Alice felt at the Mad Hatter's tea party, Amy thought. She started to laugh. Clara joined in, just a giggle at first, but soon they were both roaring with laughter, tears rolling down their cheeks.

Then Amy's laughter turned to real tears, but Clara didn't seem to notice. She stuck the end of the hotdog in her mouth, jumped up and started to dance around wildly. Round and around she whirled until she fell down dizzy on the grass. Amy could see her shoulders shaking and she wondered if she was choking, but when she went around to the other side of Clara, she saw that the hotdog had been spewed out and she was still laughing. Amy slapped her on the cheek with her open hand. Clara stopped and lay still in the grass, curled up in a fetal position with her hands tucked between her knees.

Amy was horrified at what she'd done. Clara wasn't hysterical, she was just laughing, maybe even trying to make Amy feel better by being a clown. Clara lay still, shoulders hunched as if awaiting the next blow. Amy thought her heart would break. She slumped down beside Clara on the grass and put both arms around her.

"I'm so sorry, Honey. I didn't mean to hurt you."

"It's okay. I'm stupid sometimes. Don't cry."

A long time after, when the grass grew damp and the moon shone over the Peace River, they got up in the moonlight and went to bed.

Next morning, as she stood at the counter in the little kitchen making ham sandwiches, Amy remembered last night. Some loving caregiver I am, she thought. I bet Mr. Randall never smacked poor Clara. He'd just double up on her medication. Zombies can't drive you to distraction. Or maybe he'd double up on his own meds. Amy knew she had a little bottle of valium in her make-up case, the one she took on airplane trips to keep her from trying to open the exit door and jump out just before take-off. Maybe she should take one. That would be really great. Get Clara off her medications and become addicted herself! Amy laughed and slathered some more mustard on the bread. She could do this without drugs.

She found the little styro-foam cooler in the back of the car and rinsed it out before she packed in the lunch; sandwiches, pickles, carrot sticks, and cheese and crackers for Clara, just in case she was in a 'no eat' mode. There were two cans of iced tea and a box of Mrs. Field's chocolate chip cookies. Hopefully, something would appeal to Clara's finicky taste buds.

The man who rented the boat supplied them with life jackets and worms and two rusty fishing rods covered with dried worm guts. There was also an old tackle box in the bottom of the boat, half submerged in oily water. He launched the boat for them and tied it up at the dock.
When they were ready to go, Amy made sure Clara was safely buckled into her lifejacket before she buckled up her own.

"Where's the best place to fish?" Amy asked the man.

"Well," he took a long suck on his pipe and blew the smoke out in a ring that wafted on the breeze for a few minutes, then dissipated in the air, "you could go down this way under the bridge, some folks say that's where they always catch the most. But me, I like to go out towards the mouth of the river, where the big fellas come in from the gulf to feed. I heard a guy once caught a marlin right there in front of Fisherman's Wharf on a worm and a ten-test line. Don't hardly believe it though."

He laughed as he undid the rope that held them to the dock and gave the little boat a shove with his foot. "Remember, now, hold that choke out for five seconds before you turn the key. It'll start just like billy-be-damned! Y'all have a nice day now, ladies, and don't catch any 'gators. They's a big daddy out there this year, et a few full growed dogs right offen the owner's lawns, they say."

"Thanks a lot." Amy said. She wondered if Clara had heard him, but she was busy with the container of worms. She opened it, took one out and laid it carefully in her palm. Then she started stroking it softly.

"Don't you worry," Clara whispered to the worm. "I'll look after you."

Amy pulled out the choke, waited the prescribed five seconds and held her breath as she turned the key in the ignition. After a few sputters, the engine caught with a reassuring rumble. When she put it in gear they took off at a gentle speed, heading for open water. The breeze felt good against Amy's face as the little boat cruised along. She started to relax. Clara put one hand over the side of the boat trailing her fingers in the water. Then she carefully dumped the entire container of worms overboard before Amy could stop her.

"Bye-bye," Clara said. "Y'all have a nice day."

Amy decided to make for the bridge. She really didn't want to catch a marlin. In fact, she didn't want to catch a fish at all. Gord had taught her how to bait her hook and she could even take a fish off, if it hadn't been a damn fool and swallowed the hook, but she didn't really care if she caught one or not. This trip wasn't about the fish. It was about being out on the river in the warm Florida sunshine doing something fun with Clara. And she could see that Clara was waking up a bit, looking more interested and involved. Amy felt her hopes rising once again. "Hope springs eternal..." she muttered to herself. But maybe this time things would work out well. It didn't really matter that they had no bait.

When they reached the shade of the overpass Amy cut the motor and drifted further on down the river into the grassy area where it wound around and back on itself many times. She found some bright pink rubber worms in the tackle box and threaded them on their hooks. She was quite sure that no self-respecting fish would have anything to do with them, but it was fun to dangle them in the water and feel the imaginary pull on the line when the current caught them. Clara spent most of her time reeling and unreeling the line.

9249* by Mary Haylock

"Look, I got one." She sounded excited.

"Good for you, Honey."

"Oops, he got away."

"Too bad. Was it a big one?"

"Fred likes fish."

"Well, if you catch a big one, we'll cook it up for Fred's dinner."

"Okay."

It wasn't much, but it was the closest thing to a conversation they had had for three days. The gentle rocking of the boat along with the heat and the soft sound of lapping water soon put Amy into a dreamy, half asleep state. She didn't notice how close they were getting to the shore.

As the hull of the little boat scraped on the bottom of the river, she woke up just in time to see an enormous alligator sunning himself on a sandy bank about thirty feet away. Her heart stopped beating and then set up a wild clamouring in her chest as adrenaline coursed through her body. He seemed to be asleep, still as a dead tree, but close enough to the boat that he could reach them with one or two convolutions of his gigantic tail if he felt like it.

For a minute Amy was frozen in fear. Then she reached slowly for the key in the ignition and turned it on. The engine growled, coughed a few times and died. She had forgotten to pull out the choke! With shaking hands, she yanked the button out and counted one, two three, . . . shit! The alligator's eyes opened, he blinked, his enormous mouth stretched wide to reveal rows of sharp jagged teeth. Amy tried the ignition again. Rum-rum-rum, rum-rum-rum… put-put-put, at last the engine caught. She jammed it into reverse and waited for what seemed a lifetime until the little boat slid off the sand bar and backed slowly out into deeper water.

As they moved, so did the monster on the shore. He let out a roar that shook Amy's innards and then with two great slithers of his tail he was in the water, heading right for them. Just as he was getting close, his great head disappeared under the water. Amy shoved the speed lever ahead as far as she could and they shot forward into the river, just out of reach of the beast behind them.

On and on they sped with Amy afraid to slow down or look behind. At any moment she expected the creature to launch itself out of the water onto the back of the boat where Clara was sitting, hanging on to the side with both hands. It was at least ten minutes of full out racing speed before Amy could find the courage to look behind. The alligator was no where to be seen, probably lurking under the water, no doubt disappointed that his little boat full of lunch had escaped. Amy leaned over the wheel and closed her eyes. Her heart was beating in time with her words:

"Oh God! Oh God! Oh God!" she could hardly catch her breath.

"Wheee!" Clara yelled. She put both hands straight up over her head as if she was rocketing along in a roller coaster. "Wheee!"

Amy didn't slow down until they were back in the widest part of the river where other fishing boats were anchored or drifting along in the current. Only then was she able to take a full breath. Her heart was still beating like mad, alternately fluttering and pounding in her chest. She felt sick. That enormous predator had almost caught them.

9249* by Mary Haylock

She had to get back to shore and the safety of the little cabin. When she did, she tied the boat up and took Clara and the lunch inside and shut the door. Only then did she feel safe. They ate their ham sandwiches sitting at the little table in the corner. Not much of a picnic, Amy thought. But thank God they were still alive.

Clara lay down on the bed after taking a few nibbles of her sandwich. She seemed totally unperturbed by their near disaster. Her eyes closed and she went right to sleep. Amy tried to sleep too, but she kept reliving the terrifying event in her imagination. I think I have post traumatic stress disorder, she thought to herself. Now I know what that means. She finally gave up on sleep and got out of bed. She wanted to tell someone her story, but who? It was sad to realize that no one in their vicinity would even care. The only ones who would give a shit were at home frantically wondering where they were.

That night Amy couldn't close her eyes without reliving the terror of the morning. Around three o'clock a headache came on suddenly and sent a stabbing pain through the right side of her head. It was so bad she got up and took two painkillers and lay down again, sweating and still unable to sleep. Then the pain dissolved into a kind of hot liquid inside her brain and a white shroud of brilliant light encompassed her. The last thing she heard was Clara's voice echoing in her head:

"Amy, wake up, wake up. It's time to go fishing. Amy wake up!"

9249 by Mary Haylock*

Chapter 15

Amy felt as if she were muffled in cotton wool. Her eyes opened but nothing seemed to make any sense. There were bright lights and strange unfamiliar faces looking down at her. They all seemed to be talking at once but nothing they said made any sense to her. It was all too much to comprehend so she closed her eyes and let herself drift back into the comfort of nothingness.

The next time she woke up, she managed to figure a few things out. This was a hospital, and the people were doctors or nurses. The bright lights got the better of Amy again and she tried to slide back into oblivion but this time something was stopping her. Some memory that she chased around in her mind but couldn't quite catch hold of. She was in a boat, rocking and rocking and someone else was with her. They were in mortal danger, something in the water was after them. It sent a rush of adrenaline through her, making her heart beat so hard that alarms went off and she slipped away again.

As Amy slowly regained consciousness for the third time, she heard a man's voice above her head, and the words made some sense this time.

"I think they got her here in time. Under three hours. Hopefully, there won't be too much damage. For now, just let her sleep."

"Yes, doctor." A female voice from outside her line of vision.

Who are they talking about, Amy wondered? She struggled to regain her faculties. Someone was in danger. Who was it? But the effort was too much, and she once again went blank in a world of white light. The next thing she knew she was awakened by the sound of someone screaming loudly.

"Clara! Clara!"

A nurse's face appeared and a cool hand touched Amy's forehead.

"Take it easy, dear. Clara's fine. She's out in the waiting room. Would you like to see her now?" Amy tried to nod her head and the nurse disappeared. The next face she saw was a familiar one. It was Clara. Amy tried to say something to her, but nothing came out right. Clara smiled and patted her hand.

"Hi Amy," she said softly. "Here I am. Don't worry. Everything will be all right. I`ll look after you."

Something was dreadfully wrong, Amy knew, but she couldn`t figure out what it was. All she knew was that Clara was there with her and it made her feel less afraid. She closed her eyes and slept a real sleep, not just an empty lapse into oblivion.

It was darker and quiet when Amy came around again. She could see a chair in the room and curled up under a blanket; in the chair was Clara's familiar little shape. Amy used all her strength to hang onto that image and to try to remeber. Why was she here and why was Clara sleeping in a chair?

"Clara," Amy's lips formed the word, but nothing came out. She tried again. "Clara, Clara." Finally, she heard a croak from her mouth that vaguely resembled what she was trying to say. Clara heard and woke up.

"Amy! Are you better now?" She came quickly to the side of the bed and took Amy's hand in hers. Get up now Amy. Come on. Let's go home."

Home. The word sounded strange. What was home and where was it? I am a long way from home, Amy thought, but I don't know where I am.

Clara rang for the nurse.

"Well, well. Look who's awake," the woman smiled into Amy's face while Clara fussed with straightening the sheets and tucking them in at the foot of the bed. "Can you tell me your name dear?"

"Her name is Amy. She's my friend." Clara interjected helpfully.

"Please sit down and let her tell me herself, okay?" The nurse spoke with the same tone she used to lure children into the O.R. for a tonsillectomy.

"Okay, okay." Clara sat down in the chair but kept her eyes on Amy, who was trying to remember the question the woman had asked. Then it came to her.

"Amy, my name is Amy. . . Winston." She thought it sounded right.

"Good girl. And can you tell me where you are?"

"In a h . . .hospital?" Amy wasn't altogether sure, but it seemed to be the right word.

"That's right. You are in Charlotte Regional Hospital. You were brought here yesterday by your friend over there because you had a little stroke. Do you understand what I'm saying Amy?"

"Yes, I... I.. do." She knew what the words meant, but it still didn't make much sense to her. Port Charlotte hospital was in Florida, where she used to go with Tom. No, not Tom. Someone else. Amy started to feel a headache coming on.

"My head hurts," she said.

"I'll get you something for that right away. Just close your eyes and rest now. You've been through quite a lot." The nurse went out and Clara tiptoed back to Amy's bedside. She put her hand under Amy's elbow in a very professional way and raised her into an upright position. Then she began to fluff up the pillows behind Amy's head. When she was done, she lay Amy back down carefully and pulled the blanket up to her chin, smoothing the sheet and tucking it snugly in.

"There you go," Clara said. "Now you rest up. I'll be right here."

Amy knew something wasn't quite right about this whole thing. But she was too tired to worry about it now. She closed her eyes again and drifted off. The next time she awoke she saw a man's face looming over her. He leaned forward and spoke in a very loud clear voice.

"You're going to be all right Mrs. Winston. You've had a small stroke, but I think you should make a good recovery from this little episode. We have given you some medication that should help. Now you just have to take it easy and get some rest. I'll be in tomorrow to see how you're doing."

"Thank you, doctor," Clara said from her chair.

9249* by Mary Haylock

He shot her a puzzled look and then hustled out the door fumbling with his stethoscope. Clara came to stand beside the bed. She pressed two fingers against Amy's wrist and looked up at the clock on the opposite wall. Then she nodded to herself and replaced Amy's hand on top of the blanket.

"Your pulse is just fine," she pronounced confidently.

Amy began to remember what it was that bothered her so much in her dreams. This was all wrong. Clara shouldn't be looking after her. She was supposed to be looking after Clara. It was Clara who should be in the bed. But why? She looked perfectly healthy. And Amy knew deep down that there was something dreadfully wrong in her own head.

She hadn't felt this bad since that time when she overdosed on margaritas at the Outback during happy hour. No matter how hard she concentrated, she couldn't figure out what was happening.

A tray was brought in and Clara helped Amy sit up to eat. The smell of the food nauseated her, so she turned her head away when Clara offered a spoonful of some unidentifiable brown substance.

"Come on now. Eat your dinner. That's a good girl," Clara coaxed.

When Amy refused to open her mouth, Clara ate it herself. She daintily picked at some of the other offerings and then removed the tray and went back to her chair. She opened her book and seemed preoccupied with what she was reading. But Amy had a sick feeling that something was wrong with this picture. She willed herself to stay awake and to try to think this through.

With a great deal of effort she began to remember things. Clara wasn't really reading that book. She was just pretending because as soon as she read anything, she immediately forgot what it said. Like the book about Cats. The one in the cabin. The cabin by the river where they were staying. Where they went fishing and got chased by the alligator. They were in Florida! But why?

Alzheimer's!

At last the missing pieces fell into place; Clara in the home, locked up with the daffies, the red licorice, crossing the border, the trip down here, everything came swimming slowly back into Amy's mind.

It took a few minutes before Amy realized that although she remembered quite a bit, a lot had happened that she didn't know about. Like how Clara managed to get her here and where had she been staying while Amy had been out of it. The next time the nurse passed by Amy tried to find out.

"Can you please tell me how I got here, nurse?"

"I wasn't on duty last night, but I heard that your friend here called 911 and the paramedics brought you in to emerge."

"But my friend Clara has. . . Al. . . Alzheimer's. How did she remember what to do?"

"Sometimes, in dire situations, a power kicks in that is hard to explain. Sort of like the grandmother who can suddenly lift a car off her grandson's body when he has been run over. No one really knows the strength of mind that can make a human being rise to the occasion, so to speak. But one thing for sure, you owe your friend a lot. If she hadn't called, you wouldn't be talking to me now the way you are." She smiled reassuringly at Amy.

9249* by Mary Haylock

"But who has been looking after her? Where has she been staying?"

"She refused to move from this room. We offered to put her up in the family suite down the hall, but no way. We knew she had issues of some kind, but she was determined, and you seemed to relax when she was around, so we let her stay. I think she slept in that chair last night. The nurses and the security people on the night shift kept an eye out for her. And the kitchen staff made sure she had something to eat."

"My family. . . in Canada . . .do they know?" Amy hoped they did.

"I don't know about that, but I can send in the administrator to talk to you if you feel up to it."

"Yes, yes, please." Amy started to think about the hospital bill she was racking up. She had out of country holiday coverage with her teacher's policy, but she wasn't sure it covered kidnapping.

The administrator turned out to be a young tanned fellow in an open-necked shirt and jeans.

"How can I help you, Mrs. Winston?" he asked.

"How long will I be here and how much will I owe when I'm re. . . remorsed." Amy knew that wasn't quite right, but it didn't seem to faze the young man. She braced herself for the bad news. But it was better than she thought. Her insurance plan covered her hospital stay and most of the medications they had given her. It even provided for an air ambulance to take her home if she needed it. Amy felt a great relief. At least this little fiasco wouldn't cost the children their inheritance.

Later that afternoon Amy had an unexpected visitor. She hardly recognized the man from the fishing camp who had rented them the cabin and the boat. He had shaved and was dressed up in clean pants and a plaid shirt. He came into the room, baseball cap in hand, looking slightly embarrassed. Clara jumped up out of her chair and shook his hand.

"Hi Opie!" she said. "Amy's all better now."

"I'm happy to hear that, little lady." He turned his attention to Amy. "You look a lot better than I remember," he laughed. "You were one sick puppy last time I saw you."

"What happened last night?" Amy asked.

"Well, long about three in the a.m. me and the missus were sawing logs when we heard your friend here yellin' up a storm. I thought maybe that 'gator chased you right up to your cabin. I got out of bed and put on my pants and when I got to your place, she grabbed my arm and told me to call the ambulance because you were sick. So I did, and later on, I brought some of your stuff here to the hospital."

"Thank you, Opie is it?"

"Yes ma'am."

"Thank you, Opie. I owe a lot to you. . . and to Clara."

"Hell, ma'am, I just did what the little lady here told me to do." He twirled the cap in his hand shyly.

Where did this 'little lady' come from, Amy wondered? Was this the same Clara who sat for two days in a semi-catatonic state barely eating or speaking? How had she managed to corral her faculties long enough to recognize Amy's life-threatening condition and do something about it? Amy wondered if they had put Clara into the ambulance with her and if she asked the paramedics, 'Where are we going?' until it drove them to distraction.

She had lots of time to think about these questions for the next few days as she underwent many tests and was visited by a physiotherapist, a speech therapist and even a very sweet little woman who announced herself as 'the swallowing nurse.' Clara stuck close beside her during this time, sometimes just watching and sometimes asking a pertinent question or two. Amy continued to be amazed by the change in her.

All these special people seemed quite pleased with Amy's progress and she herself felt stronger each day and more in control of her mind as well as her body. Once in a while a word escaped her, and she had to concentrate very hard to retrieve it.

"Who is the president of the United States?" asked the speech therapist.   "O…O…O'Sama," Amy knew that was wrong. "No, no, O. . O . O'Banion." Oh shit, they'd think she was nuts! She closed her eyes and tried again, "O..O. O'mambo, no, …Michelle's husband!" It was the best she could do.

9249 by Mary Haylock*

Chapter 16

When she heard the familiar voice on the other end of the phone Amy felt her throat constrict with stifled tears.

"Hi Mom, is that you? It's Tom."

"Hi, Tom. Yes, it's me. How are you?"

"Never mind me, how are you?" He was using that tight, controlled voice she knew so well when he was upset. This was not going to be easy.

"I'm doing fine, Honey. Tom, I hope you're not too . . .much mad at me. I know it was a stupid thing to do, but I had to do it. . . for Clara's sake, you know. I didn't mean to cause you guys all this. . this trouble."

There was silence for a few moments. Amy could picture her older son trying hard to understand his mother. He was so much like Gord and so little like her. It was hard for him to figure her out.

"We were all very worried, you know, when we called and called, and you weren't home yet and then we called your friend Ann from the book club and she said they hadn't gone to Ottawa at all. We came over to your place and your pills were gone and other stuff that Emma said no woman would leave behind when she left home. We called the police and they searched all over Canada for you. And then Debbie called and told us about Clara being missing from the home and we started to put two and two together. We still didn't think to look down south for you until one of the cops said, "Where's a place that your mother would know really well?" and Dave came up with Punta Gorda, so they expanded their search just before we got the call from the hospital. It's been a gruelling time for all of us, Mom. It was a really stupid thing to do." Tom's voice cracked just like it used to when he was a teenager and Amy felt the tears sliding down her cheeks.

"I know, I know. I'm so sorry to have uh. . uh. . worried you all."

"Well we're just glad you're alright, Mom. We've made arrangements to fly you and Clara home from Fort Myers airport on Air Canada in a couple of days. Davey's on the way down right now. He got a flight out of Hamilton and he'll be there later tonight. He'll look after things down there and make arrangements to get you on the plane. Then he'll drive your car back. There'll be someone on the plane with you to look after you both. Don't worry about anything. Just come home safe and sound. We all love you, Mom."

"See you soon, Tom. Give my love to. . everybody. Bye."

After she hung up the phone, Amy sat for a few minutes in silence, thinking about all the trouble she'd caused. Did she regret it? She looked at Clara who was tidying the bedside table and refilling the glass of water that was always placed there.

Clara was in her element. Happy and productive for the first time in ages. Amy wasn't naïve enough to think Clara was cured, but this little hiatus from her horrible illness seemed to have given her a new purpose. Who knows what long lasting effect it might have?

Davey showed up at the hospital later that night, looking dishevelled, as usual and tired from the long flight. His dark eyes were full of concern and he looked much older than Amy remembered. Although she tried hard to control herself, Amy burst into tears when she saw him. He didn't say anything, just came directly to the bed in three giant steps and put his arms around her. It felt so familiar, so safe, so right, that Amy just snuggled against his chest and closed her eyes. She wished she could stay there forever.

When Davey managed to disentangle himself from her embrace, he noticed Clara peeking at him from where she sat reading in her chair in the corner.

"Hi, Mrs. C. You're looking good. Nice tan you've got there."

"Thankyou, doctor." Clara smiled up from her book for a moment and then resumed her reading. Davey raised an eyebrow at Amy, who just shrugged her shoulders and smiled.

Davey looked after the hospital bill and the airport arrangements and then left to get ready for the long trek home with the PT Cruiser. Opie had offered to let him stay at the cabin for the night. He had to be back at work in four days so he couldn't stick around long. Amy hated to let him go.

"Don't worry, Ma. You'll get home before I will. I'll see you there, okay?"

"Okay, Honey. Drive carefully." Amy tried to sound cheerful even though she felt like clinging to him and begging him to stay. "Say hi to Derek and . . .Jell. . .Julie when you get home."

9249* by Mary Haylock

Opie's wife packed up the rest of their belongings in the cabin and helped Davey load them into Amy's car. She kept out some clothes and a few cosmetics and Opie delivered them to the hospital the next day. He said that Davey had paid what was owing on their bill at the fish camp before he took off. Opie didn't say how much it was, but he was smiling and cheerful so Amy figured he might have padded it a bit. She didn't really care. She would straighten things out with Davey when she got home.

On the morning of the flight Clara was quiet and withdrawn as Amy went through her usual routine of walking up and down the hall with the physiotherapist and practising with the speech therapist. Clara didn't volunteer to help, just sat quietly in her chair reading page one hundred and twenty in her Cat book.

Amy could see the brightness seeping out of Clara's eyes, the worried look creeping slowly back, and she didn't know how to stop it. She knew Clara's moment in the sun was over when the porter picked up their bags and a nurse pushed Amy's wheelchair out of the room that had been their home for the last week.

"Where are we going?" said Clara with that familiar confused look as she walked beside Amy's wheelchair to the big front door where the airport limo was waiting.

"We're going home, Honey. Really home this time." With a sigh Amy took Clara's hand. The great adventure was almost over.

An Air Canada attendant helped them board the plane and Amy was surprised to find they were in first class. They always flew economy on their trips, squeezed together in a pair of tiny seats. Clara liked to look out the window, so she always sat on the window side. Amy needed to stretch her long legs into the aisle once in a while to get the kinks out, so she would take the aisle seat. Clara would usually read for most of the trip while Amy spent a while pushing the buttons on her armrest to try to make the movie screen work. By the time she figured it out, the movie was often half over.

They always shared the food that was served on two trays jammed into the space behind the seats in front of them. Clara ate Amy's salad and Amy ate Clara's dessert.

It was a ritual that had suited them both for many years as they'd travelled the world together.

But this time was different. The seats in first class were like reclining chairs and the space between them was huge so there was lots of room for moving around. The cabin steward hovering nearby rushed over to help Amy find the right movie channel so she could watch it right from the start. Then he brought them each another free drink, something tasty with an umbrella in it. When that one was gone, he brought another.

In the middle of the movie Clara grabbed Amy's arm and pointed out the window. When Amy looked to see what Clara was so excited about, she saw a rainbow, curving through the light mist above the clouds, where the shafts of sunlight turned little droplets of water into shimmering arcs of colour. It reminded Amy of a misty morning in Delphi a few years ago, when, standing alone high up in that mystical place, she had posed a question in her head for the oracle.

"Will I be alone for the rest of my life now that Gord is gone?"

She listened but all she heard was the whispering of the wind through the pine trees. At the bottom of the hill she had run into the tour guide.

"I asked the oracle a question, but she didn't answer me." Amy told him.

9249* by Mary Haylock

The Greek guide smiled a mysterious smile. "The answer will come to you tonight in your dreams," he replied with certainty. Amy hadn't been so sure.

But the next morning, when Amy opened the curtains in their room, she had seen a double rainbow sweeping across the sky and down into the valley far below. Was this her answer. . . a message for her from the gods of Olympus? But what did it mean? At the time, it was a mystery but now Amy thought she knew the answer. It was a sign that she and Clara were bound together in a beautiful friendship, two souls united to take on the world together.

Amy and Clara watched entranced through the porthole of the plane until the rainbow dissolved slowly into the clouds. They both fell asleep over Washington DC. Next thing Amy knew they were coming in for a landing at Pearson International in Toronto. This, at last, was the end of the rainbow. But there was not likely to be a pot of gold waiting for either of them.

Amy could imagine that she was in for a family crisis meeting of some kind. They would be wondering if she was competent to live alone and look after her own affairs anymore. She had a power of attorney at home in her filing cabinet naming her son, Tom, as her designated decision maker. She had signed it, but never shown it to him. She'd have to find it quick and rip it up. If they put her in a home, she knew she'd curl up and disappear, just like Clara. What would they be thinking?

"We've got to do something about mother when she gets home, Dave. I don't think she'll be able to stay by herself anymore, you know."
"Well, Tom, maybe that's true, but let's just take it slow and see how she is when she gets here. I don't mind sleeping over at her place for a few nights this week. I'm on days and Julie says

she doesn't mind staying alone. Maybe Mom can get along with a caregiver in the daytime. Who knows? She's a tough old gal."

"Tough is one thing, but senile is another. Have you ever heard of such a hare-brained scheme as the one she thought up – rescuing Clara from the home? Debbie and the rest of Clara's girls aren't too happy about that, you know."

"I know... but a home? She'd hate it. She's always been so independent, even after Dad died."

"But she'd be safe there and you know we can't look after her twenty-four seven. You and Julie both work and so do Emma and I. Neither of us has room for her. We'd have to use one of the kids' rooms and they like to have their own space. And she really bugs them. Always boring them with her long-winded stories about the old days and trying to tell them what to do."

"I know, I know. . . but a home? You'll have to tell her, bro, I don't have the balls!"

This scenario that Amy imagined for herself was bad enough, but what would happen to Clara? Amy's eyes filled with tears as she looked at her friend snuggled into the airplane seat beside her, trusting that so long as she was there, everything was okay. Clara would be locked up and shackled again even though she had somehow been able to drag herself up out of the void she inhabited long enough to rescue Amy. She couldn't stand the thought of Clara going back there

Amy closed her eyes as the big jet sank lower and lower in the sky, dropping down toward the landing strip. She felt Clara's hand sneak into hers. They always held hands at take-offs and landings. Soft as a kitten landing in a pile of laundry the wheels of the huge plane touched down on the tarmac and rolled along at a furious clip as the pilot powered back on the engines and applied the brakes smoothly. Amy opened her eyes and looked at the buildings flying past as Clara clapped along with the other passengers, applauding the skill that had brought them down from the heavens to land gently on the earth. It would have been better if the big 747 had just slid off the end of the airstrip, Amy thought. Then it would be all over for both of them. They weren't any good to anyone else now, and they sure weren't any good for each other. It would be so easy. Just oblivion, that white nothingness that Amy had experienced when she stroked out. And best of all, they'd go together, slightly tipsy and roaring down the runway of life, hand in hand.

But it wasn't meant to be. They came to a stop and taxied back to the terminal. It seemed to take a long time, but Amy didn't mind. She wasn't looking forward to facing those relatives who'd be waiting for them. The steward asked them to remain in their seats until the other passengers had deplaned so he could help them through customs and the luggage area. Clara wanted to get out, but Amy didn't undo her seatbelt.

"Sit down, Clara. We have to wait for a few minutes."

"Get this thing off me, damn it!" Clara pulled at the belt with both hands.

"Stop it, Clara. It won't come off till it's time to go."

Clara settled back in her seat and looked blankly at Amy.

"Where are we going?"

"Right back where we started." Amy felt the tears welling up again as Clara started to sing in a melancholy little voice: *Taking a Chance on Love.*

9249 by Mary Haylock*

Chapter 17

When she was at last back home in her own condo, Amy thought back on the reunion with their families at the airport and decided that it hadn't really been that bad. There were tears and embraces and gentle scoldings from her boys and Clara's daughters, but what came through loud and clear was that their children really cared about them. When it came time to find their cars and go home, Amy gave Clara a hug and whispered,

"I'll come and see you soon, wherever you are, Honey. Okay?"

"Okay." Clara said happily.

She turned and walked away; a small gray waif sandwiched between two of her daughters with their arms around her. Amy heard her ask, "Where are we going?" She couldn't hear what they answered.

Back in her own kitchen, Amy felt very tired. It was as if the responsibility of caring for Clara was the fuel that had kept her going these past weeks, and now that she was gone, Amy just wanted to sleep. She ate a bit of the supper that her daughter-in-law, Julie, had prepared, but then her head sank down on her chest and her eyes closed. She just couldn't stay awake.

9249* by Mary Haylock

Somebody put her in her nightie and tucked her into bed, where she slept soundly for the first time in a long while. When she woke up to pee in the middle of the night, she passed the darkened living room and heard the sound of familiar snoring. It was Tom, she guessed. She wondered how he was making out on her lumpy sofa. After all, he was pushing fifty now, and probably had aches and pains of his own to deal with. She decided he was a good kid. They both were.

The family hadn't said much at supper. There had been no talk of putting her in a home, at least not that she remembered. Maybe, after she went to bed, they had discussed it privately:

"Well, she's all tucked in and starting to snore already." Emma came back to the kitchen where the rest were finishing up their dessert.
"I think she's pretty good considering what she's been through. Driving all that way and finding her way on the highways by herself. Your mother's really amazing, don't you think?" said Julie.
"Yes, she's really quite a piece of work, Tom." Emma laughed.
"I know she's done something pretty remarkable," Tom agreed, "but the fact remains, she didn't think it through, just acted on impulse and put herself and Clara in so much danger. How can we just leave her on her own? She's liable to do it again, or, God forbid, something even worse."
"Gran looked pretty glad to see us at the airport, Uncle Tom. I don't think she'll be heading out on one of her adventures again real soon." Derek poured himself another glass of wine when no one was looking and secretly drank a toast to his crazy grandmother.

When Amy finally regained consciousness it was almost noon. She woke to the smell of bacon cooking and heard Tom shuffling about in the kitchen. She wondered where he found anything that didn't have green fuzz on it after two weeks in the fridge. He must have gone out to shop.

When she found her housecoat on the back of the bedroom door and put it on, she realized that she still had a few issues with mobility. She couldn't get her arms into the sleeves of the thing.

She had to call Tom to help her. But she was able to walk to the table with the aid of her cane, and she really enjoyed the breakfast he had prepared for her; coffee, toast, eggs over easy and bacon. There was even a glass of orange juice at her place, and her pill holder sitting beside her plate. It was nice to be waited on for a change. To be the one being looked after instead of the caregiver.

Maybe there was more to this retirement home business than she thought.

But no. It was one thing to have her own child look after her. She couldn't imagine living and eating with strangers. It made her shudder to think of it. Probably some big, hairy guy would be slam-dunking her into bed at night like she'd seen once in some retirement home expose on tv. And people she didn't know would be sitting with her at dinner, stealing stuff off her plate like they did to Clara. No way. Not this old lady!

Tom stayed with her for three days and then he had to leave. She was able to get around the one-floor condo quite well on her own and Tom had shopped for her and arranged some frozen dinners in a neat stack in the freezer.

She could manage a sandwich for lunch and some cereal for breakfast. Her hands were a bit shaky, but that didn't really stop her from doing much, except putting on her lipstick, which turned out to be a clownish disaster the first time she tried, so she gave up. Tom even loosened the lids of several jars, like the peanut butter and the olives so she could manage on her own.

The whole family pitched in to help. Her granddaughter Sarah washed her hair for her and spiked it up with some kind of paste in a jar. Afterwards, she painted Amy's fingers and toenails blue while they watched a chick flick Sarah had brought with her, something about vampires.

Even Derek came by to help.

"I'm thrilled to see you, darling, but why aren't you in school?" Amy asked when her grandson appeared at her door one day, unannounced.

"I gave it up. It was stupid," he said with a rakish grin, kissing her cheek.

"Well what will you do now? You'll have to get a job." He looked at her with a horrified expression.

Oh, no, Grandma dearest. I'm going to be a recluse," he announced emphatically as he threw himself on the sofa filling it with his lanky six-foot frame from one end to the other.

"A recluse?" Amy couldn't believe her ears. "You have to do something in this world before you can become a recluse. . .. like discover the cure for cancer or write a Pulitzer prize-winning novel or something. You can't just go directly from high school to being a recluse!"

"But Grandma, aren't you the one who always said I could be anything I wanted in this world? Well, I've decided to be a recluse now while I'm young and can enjoy it. Then I'll go to work when I'm sixty-five. It makes sense, don't you see?" He laughed a

9249* by Mary Haylock

wicked little laugh and jumped up, ruffling her hair as he passed by on his way to the garage to put out her garbage.

Amy decided to enjoy all this attention while she could. She was quite sure it wouldn't last. She knew Tom was thinking about her too, but in a different way. He was the practical one, the one who would want her to be safe.

Why did younger people always want their parents to be safe, like it was the only good way to be when you got old? Who wants to be safe? You'll be safe in your grave when you die. While you still have life in your body, the thing you want to be most of all is in mortal danger! This is the feeling you get on a wild roller coaster ride like Space Mountain in Disneyland where she and Gord had taken the kids when they were young.

That's what you miss the most getting old, that adrenaline rush and feeling like your stomach has taken flight right out of your mouth. Or the choking overpowering feeling when you're in love and you can't live without each other and when you're together the passion just takes over and drowns you in your own juices. That's what old people miss!

She knew she had to play the game, though. To pretend to have learned her lesson. To never complain about anything, no matter how much it hurt or how hard it was to live alone. She had to do what pleased them on the surface so they would think she was safe, and no one would ever say to them, "How come you didn't take care of your mother? What kind of a son are you?" She had to lull them into a sense of security so she could still be a person, be herself, free and independent and able to do whatever she liked.

And of course, that had to include Clara.

9249* by Mary Haylock

Amy didn't mention Clara at all for a few weeks. She knew that she couldn't stop them from putting her back in Spring Garden Manor anyway, and she didn't want anyone to think she was the least bit concerned about Clara anymore.

Let them think she had forgotten all about her old friend, then they would relax and let down their guard. When that happened, Amy would strike again. She just didn't know how she'd do it this time, but she was still determined to try. There had to be a way.

While she waited, Amy watched videos of 'The Great Escape' and 'Prisoner of Zenda. Her mind went over and over the possibilities until she had to stop thinking because it gave her such a headache.

One thing she knew for sure, she couldn't tunnel under the Daffy ward to get Clara out. But after watching a tv show about prisoners escaping when the fire alarm rang, and all their cell doors opened up, she started to think maybe this was the answer. A false alarm. All the residents of Spring Garden herded outside in the dark while the firemen checked out the building. She and Clara slipping away in the confusion. No one would notice, except maybe Mr. Randall:

"Nurse! Nurse! Where is Mrs. Cunningham?"
"I saw her come out, Mr. Randall. I think she's over there near the hedge. Don't worry, she's with her friend."
"Not that Winston woman! I told everyone she wasn't allowed in here anymore. What's wrong with you people? Don't you remember what she did last month? When I find out who let her in, heads will roll!"
"Take it easy, Mr. Randall, your blood pressure. Don't worry, we'll find her."

9249* by Mary Haylock

"Oh shit, my grandmother is really going to kill me this time."

Amy laughed as she imagined this little scene. But it just might work. Only this time she had to think things through, plan where they were going and make sure everything was ready before they took off.

Maybe they'd go out of the country again, but this time far away. Maybe Australia or Greece. Clara had such a good time there. She'd love it. It would take some doing, but Amy felt confident she could pull it off. After all, she'd done it before. All she had to do was keep from stroking out again. But, hell, no one could tell her if that was likely to happen or when. It was just the luck of the draw, her doctor said.

Luck! That's what they needed. Just a little luck like Clara had in that Casino up north when she won the fifteen hundred dollars.

Vegas! That's where they'd go. And with Clara's luck, maybe they could win enough money to go on a cruise around the world. Amy had heard about a cruise that lasted for six months. No one would ever find them out at sea. Even if Clara got lost, she couldn't go too far. And if she decided to jump off the thing, well so what? At least she'd go quickly with her whole life passing before her eyes. All the good times they'd shared, all the countries they'd visited, all the wonderful years when the kids were little, all the high school capers and cheerleader shenanigans. If the gods of Olympus meant them to be together, who could argue with that even if it meant drowning together? Amy was sure it was the best idea she'd ever had!

When Tom came to see her unexpectedly one Friday Amy looked into his beautiful blue eyes and felt a little sad. They were just like his father's eyes. Sometimes bright blue and full of love, sometimes dark and stormy like an angry ocean. She missed Gord's eyes so much.

Looking closely, she tried to predict what it was Tom had come to talk to her about. It must be something important since he'd taken time away from his work. Amy hoped it didn't have anything to do with putting her in a home.

"Hi, Honey," she said. "Sit down. Can I get you something? A cup of tea? A beer?"

"No thanks, Mom. I can't stay away from the office too long. I just wanted to float an idea past you, see what you thought." He took off his glasses and pinched the bridge of his nose between two fingers. When he opened them, his eyes were an inscrutable turquoise. Here it comes, Amy said to herself.

"Okay, dear. Let's hear it."

"Well, Emma and I talked it over and we wondered if you'd like to come and live with us. Now, before you say no, just promise you'll think about it. Sarah is heading back to university in the fall, and her room will be empty most of the time, so she doesn't mind moving her stuff into the playroom and fixing that up for when she comes home. She actually seemed excited about it. It's a lot bigger down there and away from us so she'd like that. She could entertain her friends and we wouldn't have to listen to her god-awful music. We've thought it over carefully, all three of us, and we think this would be great for everyone. You wouldn't have to cook or clean anymore and we could help you with other stuff you need to do and best of all you wouldn't be lonely anymore, Mom."

He reached across the table and took her hand in his. "Oh, don't tell me you're not lonely a lot of the time. And besides, we'd love to have you with us. Will you at least think about it?"

9249* by Mary Haylock

Amy felt the tears gathering behind her eyes. He was so much like his father, kind and thoughtful and loving. How could she explain to him that what he offered had too high a price tag? That an end to loneliness and pain and hard work would also mean an end to her independence and freedom. What he thought of as safe, to her meant she would be removed from all the aggravations of life that let her know she was still alive, still herself, still a small but integral part of the universe. She couldn't do it. Not yet. Not until she had to. And then, of course, there was Clara.

"Thank you, Honey. I'll think about it. I promise. I love you, Tommy."

"Love, you too, Mom." Some day, when she was long dead, and he was an old man himself, he would understand why her answer had to be no.

9249* by Mary Haylock

Chapter 18

It was a month since she had seen Clara when Amy got a phone call from Clara's daughter one night after supper. She recognized the voice immediately and the caution flag went out.

"Amy, hi. It's Debbie Cunningham."

"Hi, Debbie. How are you?"

"I'm good. How about you? Tom says you've recovered really well from your stroke." *So, they'd talked about her behind her back.*

"Yes, I'm doing just fine, thanks. I've had a lot of scans and tests and stuff and they seem to think I'm doing okay." Amy waited. She didn't want Debbie to think she was too interested in finding out about Clara.

"We went to see mom today and she's settling in quite well. She has a different room and for a while she was a bit confused about that. Sometimes we'd find her in someone else's bed when we visited." Debbie gave a little half-hearted laugh. "But she's better about that now and seems to know where she belongs. I thought you might want to know. It's room 114, just a few doors down from where she was before."

9249 by Mary Haylock*

Amy's mind was racing. Clara was still in the Daffy ward, but in a different room, 114. She reached for a pen and wrote the number on the back of her hand. Why were they telling her this unless they wanted her to visit Clara again? Did it mean that all was forgiven? Amy wasn't sure, but it sounded hopeful. She could hear no trace of anger in Debbie's voice.

"Are you still there, Amy?"

"Yes, I was just writing down the room number in case I visit her again some time. Do you think I should? Will she know me?"

"Oh, yes. She asked for you the other day. 'Where's Amy?', she said. "I'm sure she'd like to see you. Just stay out of Mr. Randall's way. You're not his favourite person, you know."

I'll just bet I'm not, Amy thought. And when I get Clara out again, I'll be on his most wanted list for sure. Just wait till I get finished with the little fucker.

"Thanks for telling me, Debbie. Maybe I'll stop by to see her some time this week. I'll let you know how she is. Bye for now." Amy hung up the phone and looked at the calendar. She'd have to stop wasting time and get moving on her five-alarm fire plan.

When the taxi pulled up in front of Spring Garden Manor the next day, Amy had a moment of indecision before she stepped out. On the way there she'd thought about just letting things be, about going to live with Tom and having him look after her for the rest of her days and about just visiting Clara once or twice a year. She would probably get so she didn't recognize her anyway and it wouldn't be so hard to stay away. It would mean an end to her loneliness and the feeling she wasn't good for anything anymore. She could help Emma do the dishes and the laundry, anything that didn't require bending over too far or lifting something heavy. And she'd see more of Sarah. They could look at some of the old family pictures that Amy had stashed away in tubs in the basement. She could tell her granddaughter who the people were smiling out at them from these old prints; her great-grandmother, and grandfather and even pictures of Gord when he was young. Sarah was so little when he died, she'd hardly remember him at all.

"Who's this, Grandma? He's a good-looking dude."
"That's your grandfather, Thomas Gordon Winston. Everyone called him Gord. Do you remember him at all?"
"I think so. Once he taught me how to cut my mashed potatoes in squares."
"That's him."
"Is this your wedding, Grandma?"
"Yes. That's me. My dress cost twenty dollars. A friend of my mom's made it for me. It was beautiful."
"Who's this little cutie?"
"That's Clara. She was my maid of honour. She looks so young, so beautiful."
"You look really pretty too, Grandma."
"Don't sound so surprised."

Maybe she could even take a few little day trips to the casino in Niagara Falls or to the Shaw Festival on a bus full of other old farts. It was a tempting idea. Without Clara she had no one to do anything with. She was tired of facing the world on her own, pretending to be this independent liberated woman who could look out for herself. It would be so nice just to relax and let go.

But something stood in her way. It was the idea of Clara, being locked up that way. It just wasn't right. It wouldn't let Amy rest. She was obsessed with the unfairness of it all.

Amy paid the taxi driver and gave him a small tip. She hated the idea of not having her own car, but Tom had taken it to the shop to have it over-hauled after the long trip to Florida. She hoped it wouldn't be long until she was back behind the wheel again.

Until then she had to rely on her boys, or one of the grandkids to ferry her around. They were never there when she needed them, so it was easier to take a cab. It killed her to pay the fare and then a tip on top of that, and she never quite knew how much to give the driver. If he chatted with her or opened her door or something, she gave him a bit extra.

Paying bills was man's work, after all. She hated having to figure out the tax on a restaurant bill, so she knew how much to give the waitress. The first time she'd gone out for a meal after Gord died, she'd walked out of the restaurant chatting with Clara and left the unpaid bill on the table. It was something she'd never had to worry about before. The waiter ran after her out into the mall. Amy had never felt so alone in her life.

When she got to the entrance of Spring Garden Manor, Amy stopped in front of the door. She hoped the code was the same as before, 1234*. She leaned down and pressed the numbers and was relieved to see the green light above the pad go on. The door opened and she slipped inside, hoping to avoid the woman sitting at the reception desk. Not so.

"Hi, Mrs. Winston. We haven't seen you for a while. How are you?" It was the loud-mouth volunteer who had given her a hard time about getting Clara drunk.

"Hello." Amy made it short. She didn't want to get into a conversation with the woman.

9249* by Mary Haylock

"Mrs. Cunningham's in a new room now. Just a minute and I'll look up the number for you."

"I know where she is, thank you. Her daughter told me." Amy hurried away before the woman could open her register. She hoped the old cow wouldn't call Mr. Randall and tell him she was back in the building.

There was a singsong in the large gathering room, and someone was banging out old tunes on the piano in the corner. Several residents sat in the comfortable chairs and sofas scattered about the room and were singing along to the music. Amy looked at the faces to make sure Clara wasn't there. It was just the kind of thing she'd love. But there was no sign of her. Amy passed on through the dining room, smiling and nodding as she went. When she got to the big steel door to the Daffodil ward she had to think for a moment. 9249*... The door opened and Amy went through. She walked down the hallway until she found Room 114.

Before she knocked, she stood and thought for a moment. She could still turn around and get out before Clara saw her. She would never know she'd been there. Hell, she'd never know five minutes later even if she did go in. But somehow that wasn't an option. Amy knocked softly and opened the door. As usual, curtains covered the large window and it was semi-dark inside. Amy could make out a bed in the corner of the room and someone under the covers. She hoped it was Clara.

"Is that you, Toots?" Amy opened the curtains and the body on the bed gave a moan and turned over. "Come on, get up. It's me, Amy."

"Amy? Is that you?"

"Yes, it's me. Get up and say hello."

"Hello."

"I've missed you. It's been a long time." Amy gave her a hug.

"Where are we going?" Clara sat on the edge of the bed looking up at Amy, her expression cloudy.

"Oh, no you don't. Don't start that again."

"What?" Clara looked puzzled.

"That, 'Where are we going?' crap."

"I don't know."

"What don't you know?" Amy was getting confused.

"I don't know where we're going." She had only been in the room for five minutes and already Clara was making her head spin. "Where do you want to go?" Amy asked.

"Florida."

Amy had expected to hear the familiar 'home'. But Clara's answer came as a shock. My god, did she remember? "Why do you want to go there?"

"Where?"

"Florida."

"Fred's there."

9249* by Mary Haylock

I can't do this, Amy thought. I don't know where I am anymore. She sat down heavily in the chair by the window. There was a soft rap on the door and Amy opened it. It was Mr. Randall.

"Hello, Mrs. Winston. How are you?" He sidled into the room, looking around at everything before he spoke to Clara in a louder tone of voice. "How are we today, Mrs. Cunningham?" Clara just looked at him blankly. He turned his attention back to Amy.

"Mrs. Winston, I'm glad to see you back at Spring Gardens. I'm sure Mrs. Cunningham has missed seeing you. Have you recovered from your little problem?"

"Yes, pretty much." Amy was wary of this unexpected friendliness.

"Well, I have a proposition for you. May I call you Amy?" She nodded and he went on. "We are running perilously short of volunteers these days, Amy, and we were wondering if you would consider helping us out. Since you're often here anyway, perhaps we could prevail upon you to visit in a slightly more official capacity."

Amy couldn't believe her ears. What was this oily little bastard up to, she wondered? She had expected him to ban her from the premises, but instead he seemed to be inviting her into the inner workings of the place. She remembered the old saying, 'Keep your friends close and your enemies even closer'. Maybe this was the tactic he was using. Perhaps he was smarter than she thought.

"For instance, Amy, your friend Clara would enjoy the singalong in the Tulip room today very much. Unfortunately, we can't spare a volunteer to watch over her out there. She really enjoys music as you know, and she can sing like an angel. And she's the hit of our Friday night dances. All the guys want her for a partner." He reached for Clara's hand and she simpered up at him.

Amy was flabbergasted. Friday night dances? This was the first she'd heard of them. But she remembered from high school how Clara loved to dance. In gym class they often danced but there were no boys, of course, so she and Clara danced together. Amy had to lead because she was taller. It was good practice for the sock hops that were held every month in the gym. All the boys liked to dance with Clara while Amy usually held up the wall with the other ugly ducklings. Once in a while some tall, gangly guy would get up the nerve to ask her to dance and she usually stepped all over him and had nothing interesting to say. When the song was over, he would put her back on the wall and never come that way again.

But Clara would snuggle herself into whoever she was dancing with, and they'd both close their eyes and go off to dreamland together with Kay Starr singing 'Wheel of Fortune'. She was something else, that Clara. And here she was, sixty years later, still working her magic on the old boys in Spring Gardens.

"Just what are you suggesting, Mr. Randall?" Amy asked.

"I'm asking you to become a volunteer in our little family. You know the routines pretty well, and you could spend as much time with Clara here as you liked. Then, when she was at painting class or pottery or out for lunch with the group, you could maybe give us a hand at the desk or in some other way. We'd be ever so grateful for the help and you could set your own hours of course. We'd even be happy to help with your transportation. We have a van that picks up some of our volunteers who don't drive. What do you say, Amy? Can we count on you?" He seemed to be in earnest.

"I'll think about it, Mr. Randall."

9249* by Mary Haylock

He went to the door and opened it. "Call me Randy. That's what they call me most of the time, except when Granny's around." He winked at Clara, went out and closed the door.

Amy couldn't believe how he'd come across as such a nice personable young man. Maybe she'd been wrong about him all along. Maybe she was wrong about Derek too. In fact, it was possible she'd been wrong about a lot of things. Maybe when she kept finding Clara in bed, it was because she was tired from all the activities the home apparently provided for her. Fun things, like singing and dancing and painting. Things that were probably a lot better for an old lady than being chased by alligators.

9249* by Mary Haylock

Chapter 19

It took a while, but eventually Amy figured out that her car was not coming back. Whenever she asked about it, Tom was evasive, citing a variety of different ailments that required fixing; the brakes, the transmission, the tires. Finally, Derek blurted out the truth on one of his visits.

"Thanks for the wheels, Granny," he said as he opened the cupboard doors in Amy's kitchen, searching for something to eat.

"What wheels?" Amy was on full alert.

"Dad told me I could likely have the PT now that you don't need it anymore." He stacked up a pile of saltines and proceeded to apply a layer of butter between each one. When the stack threatened to topple over, he opened his mouth wide and shoved the whole tower inside.

"He did, did he? Well that's news to me. Sorry, kiddo, but I need my car to get around. You'll have to come out of seclusion and get a *job*. Then you can buy your own car. Sorry to use the *j* word. I didn't mean to shock you." She'd have to give Davey a piece of her mind about this.

"No sweat, Gran. I thought you were okay with it." He opened the fridge and took a swig out of the milk container. "Dad says you can't drive anymore because of your stroke. Your license has been revolted or something. Don't worry, though. I'll be around to drive you wherever you want to go, just like a chauffeur. It'll be fun, Gran. I got my license last month, and I'm a great driver. I only got three parking tickets so far."

Amy was in shock. Revoked? She opened her purse and checked to see if her license was still there. The little plastic sleeve where she kept it was empty. Little by little Amy started to think about some of the strange things that had happened lately. Like the recent weekly visits by her family members.

When she looked back through her calendar, she could see that they were obviously scheduled, not just happening in a random way. Monday was Derek, Tuesday, Emma and on through the week. One of them came every day to check on her and they each had a special day assigned.

In a sudden panic, Amy remembered the power of attorney in her filing cabinet. She searched everywhere, finally collapsing in tears when she realized it was gone.

They were gradually taking away her freedom, encroaching on her territory when she wasn't around and helping themselves to her belongings and she couldn't do a thing about it. She had signed that damned thing. She felt like Scrooge in A Christmas Carol, when he saw his housekeeper selling his bed curtains before he was even dead.

Amy wasn't about to take this lying down. She had to do something, but what?

Tom now had the power to put her away somewhere to keep her safe, like Clara. She had to be careful not to give him any reason for doing that. The family was obviously together in this. They'd back Tom up, and her life would be over.

9249* by Mary Haylock

Thank God for grandchildren. If it weren't for Derek's stupidity, she'd never have known how close she was to being put out of her misery forever. When she confronted Tom on Friday, which Amy had come to realize was his day, he sat her down and took her hand in his.

"Mom, you know I would never use that power of attorney unless I had to. Why didn't you show it to me before? Don't you trust me? If you had another stroke and couldn't communicate, I wouldn't have known it was there. I found it by chance when I was looking for your income tax receipts, and I thought I'd better keep it somewhere where I could get my hands on it quickly if I needed to. There's a medical power of attorney too. Did you remember making one of those?"

Amy looked into his eyes, so full of love and concern and she felt bad about her doubts. He would never hurt her on purpose. She knew that.

"I don't want to go to a home, Tom. I want to stay here as long as I can. But I don't want to be a burden to you and Davey either. Just keep me in the loop, will you. I think I'll know when it's time to pack it in." She tried to keep the tears from spilling out and running down her cheeks where he would see them. She'd caused him enough grief already.

"And when it is time, Mom, there's still the option of staying with me and Em. We're open to that idea, don't forget. But we want you to be happy and independent for a long time. We all do."

How did this situation come about so quickly Amy wondered? It seemed like such a short time ago that she was in charge not only of her own life, but of her family too. Now they were the ones who could make decisions about her that affected her very survival. They could instruct the medical people not to feed her or ask them to pull her plug. She'd certainly be wary if she saw any of them near the life-sustaining equipment when she was in the hospital on her last legs. She could picture a visit from Derek:

"Hi Gran. I hear you're checkin' out soon. Sorry about that. What are all these machines here for?

Hey, that's sick. Listen to the beat drop: Cachunka, cachunka, cachunka. . . Mind if I turn it up a bit? Oops. Sorry Gran. It seems to have gone off when I tripped over this freakin 'cable. Gran. . . Gran? . . Gran!"

That certainly wasn't the way Amy had planned it. She wanted to go like her Aunt Mandy, propped up by satin pillows in her bed at home, looking serene and ethereal at ninety-four. She remembered her aunt's eyes sweeping across the faces of family and friends who had gathered to say goodbye to her. She took for one last look at each of them, silently burning their features into her memory before she drifted painlessly away to the soft sound of their weeping. Why couldn't it be that way for her?

Better yet, Gord should be there to hold her in his arms, letting his tears run unabashedly down his cheeks as she looked up at him wanly, told him she loved him and lowered her eyelids for the last time, long dark lashes resting gently against her pale cheeks. Greta Garbo in Camille.

That was how she'd pictured it when she married him. He wasn't supposed to go first and leave her to the wolves. Now here she was at seventy-five trying to fend for herself in a world where anyone over sixty is redundant and expendable.

In the meantime, she had Clara to worry about too. Amy had been mulling over Mr. Randall's invitation to join the volunteers at Spring Garden Manor. When she found out about her license being taken away, she decided to do it. She'd let them pick her up once or twice a week and take her there. It was a way to spend her time now that she was carless. And she could still keep an eye on Clara and plan the great escape. It might be a bit more difficult, though, without wheels.

The first time she showed up for duty Mr. Randall seemed pleased to see her. "Welcome, Amy," he gushed. "I'm so glad you decided to join our little group. My secretary will give you some papers to fill out, just routine information so we can run a police check, you understand. Once that's done, Vera will help you make up a schedule that suits you. I do hope you enjoy your time with us and thank you for helping out. We really appreciate our volunteers so much."

I'll bet you do, you little cheapskate. Amy thought. It saves you a lot of money for paid help. But she had to admit that Mr. Randall did sound sincere in his appreciation.

In truth, she enjoyed her time at Spring Garden Manor.

Although Clara was still in the Daffodil ward, now that Amy was with her, she spent a lot of time with the Tulip folks in painting and pottery classes. She didn't communicate much with the others but seemed to enjoy working beside them and listening to their conversation. At least they weren't just hanging there in their wheelchairs like the Daffies.

Amy stood beside her watching one day as Clara attacked her easel, making bold blue strokes with her brush on the white canvas.

"What are you painting, Honey?" Amy asked."

"I don't know," Clara shrugged her shoulders and squeezed some more azure #3 out of the tube onto the palette in her left hand.

"It looks a bit like water. Is it water, Clara?"

"I went for a ride on the water." She frowned at the picture and made a few more slashes at it.

"Where did you ride on the water?" Amy hoped she was remembering their wild adventure in Florida.

"What water?" Did I spill it?" Clara sounded worried.

"Never mind, it's okay. Paint away, Grandma Moses."

"I'm done now." Clara put her brush in the jar of water and set her palette down on the table beside her. Most of the canvas was still in pristine condition with just a few swipes of blue here and there.

"Is this all you're going to do?" Amy asked.

"It's finished." Clara started to wipe her hands on her jeans.

"This gives a new meaning to minimalist," Amy mumbled, disappointed that Clara had given up so soon.

The teacher walked over and looked at Clara's work. "I like this shade of blue, Clara. It's very pretty. What are you going to paint now?" As the teacher spoke, she put the palette back into Clara's hand and took the brush out of the jar of water. Clara took it and swirled it in the red paint.

9249* by Mary Haylock

"This is the boat," Clara smiled at the instructor, who nodded her approval and moved off to chat with another student. Amy watched Clara concentrating on her creation.

Amy remembered that the boat they had rented in Florida had been painted red around the gunwales. She could picture Clara's small hands gripping the wood as they made their wild escape from the alligator. The stripes of red didn't look much like a boat, but maybe this was as much remembering as Amy could hope for.

The first time Amy went out in the evening to one of the dances at Spring Garden Manor she didn't know what to expect. She was in for a surprise. The bus that picked her up was a large touring bus with comfortable cushioned seats, and Clara was already there waiting with an empty seat on the aisle next to her.

Residents and caregivers and volunteers were all there mixed together and there was an atmosphere of excitement and anticipation in the buzz of conversation. When she got on, the driver announced that this was their last pick-up and they were ready to hit the trail. Amy was surprised to see that the driver was Mr. Randall himself.

"Are you ready?" he yelled into the loudspeaker.

"We are ready!" The passengers yelled back.

Music poured from the sound system and soon the bus was rocking with the big band sound of Glenn Miller. Clara bounced happily in her seat, singing at the top of her lungs.

When they arrived, Amy was amazed to see that their destination was Alexander's Banquet Centre, a high-class beautifully appointed place that was a favourite venue for visiting celebrities when they were in town. Other buses from other retirement homes in the city were parked in front disgorging their occupants, most of whom were in varying states of decrepitude, but all apparently looking forward to an evening of dancing; wheelchairs, walkers, oxygen tanks and all. Mr. Randall manoeuvred the bus into place right in front of the main entrance and the Spring Garden folks eagerly alighted, the able-bodied helping the incapacitated. They proceeded *en masse* under a canopy to the big double doors.

Clara smiled and waved at everyone as though she were a visiting superstar walking the red carpet. She looked particularly nice, Amy thought. Someone had helped her dress up in a pink sweater set and her hair had been done in pretty soft curls that emphasized her blue eyes and gave her face an elfin look. A trace of pink blush lent some colour to her cheeks and made her eyes look alive and sparkling.

It was obvious she could hardly wait for whatever was about to happen. Amy wondered if she knew, since she hadn't once asked where they were going.

Inside the ballroom there were tables and chairs set up like an old-fashioned nightclub from a movie set. Shades of *Casablanca*. There was even a black pianist entertaining them as they came in.

"Play it again, Sam," Clara grinned as she went by. He laughed right back and started to play *As Time Goes By*. On the bandstand eight middle-aged musicians were tuning up their instruments. *Mason and the Trowels*, the sign in front of them announced.

Mr. Randall led his Spring Gardeners to a group of tables near the dance floor and everyone sat down. Amy found herself seated with Clara and Mr. Randall's grandmother, an attractive well-dressed woman about her own age, and several residents of the Tulip ward whom she had come to know. She recognized the art teacher and the husband of one of the Daffies. Mr. Faithful, the staff called him, because he came to feed his wife every single evening even though she didn't have a clue who he was.

When the band struck up 'Take Me Out to the Ballgame', Clara stood up and looked around, smiling. She waved at a dapper little gray-haired man at one of the nearby tables who came over and took her hand.

"Would you like to dance, my dear?" he said, making a courtly bow.

"You bet," Clara answered, half pulling him out onto the dance floor.

It was the last Amy really saw of her for most of the night. Oh, she saw her, but from a distance, snuggled up to some older man in her inimitable Clara way, eyes closed, hanging on for dear life. And whatever man she was with seemed to be loving it.

As usual, no one asked Amy to dance. Except Mr. Randall. When his Grandmother gave him a jab in the ribs and surreptitiously jerked her head in Amy's direction, he stood up reluctantly, clicking his heels together.

"Would you do me the honour, Mrs. Winston?" His face was red, and he kept his eyes averted. She decided to take pity on him.

"Thank you, Randy, but my hip has been bothering me today. Perhaps another time." She smiled at his obvious relief.

On the way home it was quiet except for the music coming from the bus speakers.

This time it was Moonlight Serenade, an appropriate tune since the moon was full and clearly visible in the night sky.

Most of the residents were nodding in their seats. It was almost midnight, well after their normal bedtime at the home. Amy and the other volunteers were dozing too. It had been a wonderful evening of music and memories. She was sorry it was over.

Randy had turned off the interior lights of the bus as they cruised along the deserted streets, but Amy could see Clara curled up beside her, when every once in a while, a stream of light from a lamp post outside fell across her face. She looked peaceful and content. The worried frown that usually creased her forehead was smoothed out now. The corners of her mouth, so often turned down lately, were curled up in a wisp of a smile, just the way Amy remembered her when they were young girls.

She looks about twelve, Amy thought. I wonder what she dreams about. Probably not about what happened tonight. That would be too recent for her memory to handle. But maybe the evening would have triggered a pleasant remembrance of some time long ago, when she was a young girl, just learning to dance and the world was waiting for her to make her entrance.

Chapter 20

That night Amy dreamed a strange and familiar dream. She had just bought a new house, but she had never seen it inside. When she finally got the key and opened the front door, she found herself in a long hallway with closed doors leading to many different rooms. As she opened the doors one by one, she discovered to her delight that the rooms were filled with beautiful and expensive antiques. She hadn't expected to find so many treasures in her new home.

But when she got to the last door, something made her hesitate with her hand on the knob. It was a feeling of horror that engulfed her for no apparent reason. Still, despite her brain telling her not to, she felt compelled to open the door. When it swung in on its hinges, she saw a set of stairs leading down to a dark and forbidding basement. There was something lurking down there that was so ghastly, so menacing that she somehow knew if it got hold of her, she would come to a gruesome end. Amy gathered all her strength and slammed the door shut. Then she woke up.

It was dark in the room and Amy felt the fear thundering through her body. She tried to sit up in bed but somehow couldn't move. She tried to call out, but her voice was stuck in her throat. Panic set in and Amy thought for a moment that she had been caught by the evil force in the basement. Then she realized that this was not a dream. Her heart was beating wildly in her chest, threatening to explode, when suddenly there was light in the room, and she could see someone opening the curtains covering a big window on the far wall.

It was Clara! She turned and walked back toward the bed, peering at Amy.

"Are you awake now, sleepyhead?" She smoothed the hair back from Amy's damp forehead and leaned over to kiss her lightly on the cheek.

Amy still couldn't answer or move one of her arms. The other hand reached out for Clara and grabbed hold of her shirt.

"It's okay. I'm here. I'll look after you." Clara's voice was soothing as she uncurled Amy's fingers and placed her hand back on the bed. "It's time for breakfast now. You wait here and I'll get the tray."

Amy's brain was spinning. It was all wrong. She was somehow in Clara's bed, unable to move or talk and Clara was looking after her. What the hell was going on?

Later, Amy wasn't sure if it was minutes or hours, she found out what had happened.

Mr. Randall stood beside the bed with Clara and he tried to make her understand.

"Mrs. Winston. . . Amy," he said. Do you know who I am?"

Amy managed to nod her head yes.

"Good, good," he smiled down at her. "You're here with us at Spring Garden Manor now. Do you understand?"

Once again Amy nodded. But why was she in bed? That she didn't understand. It was too much of an effort to ask him, so she closed her eyes, hoping he would go away. But she could still hear his voice. She tried harder to make sense of what he was telling her.

"You've had another little stroke, Amy, and your sons decided to bring you here to recuperate. This is the Anemone wing. We look after short term patients here. They thought it would be nicer than the hospital for you since you know all of us and of course your friend Clara here is close by and can visit you every day until you're better. We have physical therapists who will be able to help you, and your doctor feels you should be able to gain control of your walking and speaking in time. I'll leave you to rest now and I hope you'll be happy during your stay with us. We're going to take good care of you." He smiled kindly at her, patted her hand and left.

Amy tried to digest this information. It seemed impossible that she had come to this state without even being aware of it. The more she tried to remember what had happened to her, the more frustrated she became. She felt a tear tracing a path down her right cheek.

"Don't cry, Amy." Clara said as she pressed a tissue gently against Amy's face. "I'm right here with you."

Amy had lots of time to think about things. She knew she was in pretty bad shape, but the irony of the whole situation was not lost upon her. Here she was in bed, physically incapacitated to the extent that she needed help to do everything, while Clara, mentally incapacitated as she was, managed to get around just fine.

She did indeed look after Amy to the best of her ability. There were times when Clara looked at her blankly and sat in the chair beside Amy's bed reading page one hundred and twenty in her Cat book over and over again, but other times she bustled about the room straightening things on the night table and smoothing the sheets. As Amy regained some of her ability to speak, they even had a conversation or two:

"Do you have to pee?" Clara asked.

"No. What time is it?"

"I can't tell time."

"Yes, you can. Tell me." The clock was out of sight above Amy's bed. She pointed to it. Clara looked up.

"Time to go, I guess." Clara shrugged her shoulders and continued folding Amy's housecoat from the back of the chair.

"Where are we going?" Amy asked.

"Out for lunch." Clara said.

"Where?" Amy was puzzled.

"Where what?"

"Where are we going for lunch?"

"Are we going out for lunch?"

"You're crazy, Clara." Amy couldn't help but laugh. Clara joined in. They laughed until the tears rolled down their cheeks, silently, helplessly, egging each other on every time they looked at each other. Maybe I'll die laughing, Amy thought. That'd be a good way to go.

As the weeks passed, Amy regained strength in her left arm and leg and finally one day was able to walk with the aid of a walker, ten steps down the hall of the Anemone Ward. Everyone cheered, Clara loudest and longest of all.

Amy could speak also but found that her ability to retrieve the correct word was even more impaired than before. "Bring me my hairbrush" somehow came out, "Brush me my hair banner." The amazing thing was that Clara seemed to know what she meant.

There were tiny improvements in Clara's memory that Amy noticed over the many weeks they spent together. One day, Amy decided to see if Clara could still play cards. Maybe that ability was on a separate disk in Clara's brain, like the music one.

It started off well with Clara automatically shuffling the deck that Amy handed her. But when it came to dealing the cards, she did it backwards.

"Let's play 'Snap'. Turn the cards over and if your card marches. . ... matches mine, yell 'snap'", Amy instructed.

Clara turned her whole pile over on the table and yelled, "Snap!"

"No, not all at one. Once at a time. Ready? Okay, here we go again." Using her good hand, Amy turned her card over with an exaggerated slowness. Clara followed her example.

"Snip," Clara yelled.

"No, they don't much. They have to be the same. Like if I have a king, and you have a king. Like that, Okay?"

"Okay," Clara agreed. Amy turned her card slowly again. So did Clara. Two tens.

Amy waited to see what Clara would do. She looked at the cards and said nothing.

"Say snap, Clara. Look, the cards are the same."

"No, they're not. Mine is red and yours is black."

Most days Clara pushed Amy around the manor in a wheelchair. With her good hand, Amy could push the buttons to allow them to move from one area of the Gardens to another. Now she knew why the keypads were placed at such a low level. It was for people in wheelchairs, like her.

There were many sections to the building which she hadn't been aware existed. In the Lilac wing, Amy discovered a well-stocked library and a workout room with a few simple machines. There was a ping-pong table and, on a shelf, a little cage full of numbered balls for calling bingo. No matter how often they visited, Clara always headed for the small equipment shelf.

"Let's play ball," she'd say, choosing the same pink rubber ball every time.

"Okay, but go easy." Amy would brace herself for Clara's famous chest pass. Sometimes she could get her hands up in time, but most often it hit her in the face.

"Sorry," Clara would say with a mischievous look.

"You're not sorry one bit. Let's go."

"Where are we going?'

"Take me over there to the drawer. . . door."

"Are you mad?'

"No." Amy could never stay mad at Clara for long.

On one of their walkabouts, Amy discovered a locked door with no keypad. There was a window in the door and when Clara pushed her closer, Amy could see a large swimming pool with a hot tub to one side. The air had a chlorine smell. Inside, one of the volunteers was leading a class of residents in some water exercises. The old folks were fitted with flotation belts and webbed gloves and they were trying hard to keep up with their young instructor, their flabby flesh flapping in time to her rhythmic counting:

"One and two and three and four. . . jumping jacks. . . and just two more. . . and seven and eight. Good work."

It looked like fun. Maybe she could ask if she and Clara could go to this class when she got a bit more mobile.

The most painful thing for Amy during her convalescence was to look in the mirror and see the drooping eyelid and sagging skin on the left side of her face, where a cold numbness had taken over. When visitors came, she sat with her hand covering her cheek, propping up the flaccid, unfeeling flesh.

One day in painting class, when Clara finished her piece, she turned it around so Amy could see. It was unmistakably a portrait of Amy, wilted face and all, reminiscent of a Picasso she remembered having seen in a museum somewhere. The teacher thought it was quite good and hung it in the hall with some of the more stellar examples of her pupils' endeavours. Clara seemed pleased.

"Look, Amy. It's you."

"Yah, right. Thanks a lot."

9249* by Mary Haylock

"Don't you like it?" Clara looked crestfallen.

"Oh sure, I like how I look, all droopy, with one eye up and one eye down here.

"I think you're beautiful," Clara touched Amy's face gently with the tips of her small fingers. "You were always the beautiful one, so tall and willowy."

"Thank you, Clara." Amy was genuinely astonished. It was a rare occasion when Clara connected the past and present as she had just done. Maybe they were really doing each other some good. Amy knew for sure she would be terribly lonely without Clara's constant although sometimes frustrating company.

Amy's family came to visit by turns, sticking pretty much to the same schedule they'd had before. But the grandchildren were her favourites. They showed no abhorrence for the place or for their grandmother's somewhat altered looks. She liked it when they came together to visit. It made for a lively afternoon.

"Hey, Gran, how's it hangin'?" Derek would kiss her on the cheek and then do a headstand on her walker, balancing his six-foot body upside-down in the corner of the room. Then he'd fiddle with the gears on her wheelchair, often taking himself for a wild ride down the corridors of the Anemone ward. "Look, Gran. I can show you how to pop a wheelie on this crate if you like. Wow, this is awesome."

"Knock it off, moron." Sarah was one month older, and she liked to keep him under control. "I brought some new nail polish, Grandma. See? I'm wearing it. It's the latest thing. Vampire Black. Let's put some on your toes. It'll look rad."

"They'll think I have grenadine. . .gonorreah. . .oh shit!" Amy laughed at herself.

9249* by Mary Haylock

But she was getting better with words most of the time. And although she had a wheelchair and walker in the room, she often just used the cane that was propped up against the chair. She was getting better every day. Soon maybe she could go back home. But what would happen to Clara? She couldn't bear the thought of leaving her. When Tom came one Friday, they discussed the possibility.

"I guess you're getting anxious to go home, Mom," he said.

"I'd like to see the place, Tom, but I think I'd really miss Spring Gardens." It just popped out of her mouth, surprising both of them.

"Wow. I never thought I'd hear you say that. That's good to know because we were talking about arranging for you to stay here. Mr. Randall has an opening in the Tulip ward, and you could have a room there. It's a double, so we thought maybe you and Clara could stay together. She'd be okay if you were there to watch out for her. What do you think?"

"That might just work out, Tom. I'll have to think about it." Amy had to admit to herself that she enjoyed the meals and activities and the company. She certainly hadn't been lonely since coming here. And Clara would be free of the depressing D̲affies if she could stay with Amy in the Tulip ward.

Amy knew if she had another stroke it would likely be impossible to get back into Spring Gardens, and she'd be alone in some strange facility. Maybe this was the best way to go. On her own terms. Amy smiled as she glanced at the glass enclosed fire alarm in the hallway outside her room. After all, if it didn't work out, there was always Plan B. Fire in the Hole.

Later that evening, Amy discussed the move with Clara as they sat watching reruns of Golden Girls on tv.

9249* by Mary Haylock

"How'd you like it if I came here to live?" Amy said.

"I like it here."

"I know. That's why I'd like to live here too. What do you think?"

"I think . . . yes." Clara nodded emphatically.

"We could stay together in the same room if you want. Would you like that?"

"What?"

"If you and I were broom mates . . . groom mates. We could have a bigger room with two beds, and we could eat together and do stuff and go places. What do you say?"

"Okay." No hesitation. Clara got up from her chair and turned at the door to look back at Amy with a puzzled look on her face.

"Where are we going?"

"God only knows, Clara," Amy started to laugh. "God only knows."

9249* by Mary Haylock

AFTERWORD by the Author

After my husband passed away, I spent the next ten years travelling the world with my childhood friend, Marylou. We had many wonderful trips together, but gradually I began to notice Marylou was becoming very forgetful.

Before long, Marylou was in a nursing home, and after one little unsanctioned trip into the outside world, she was moved to the lock-downward and fitted with an ankle bracelet that set off alarms when she tried to. Needless to say, she is the inspiration for my story. Much of it is true, but the basic idea of rescuing her is, I must confess, wishful thinking. Sad as this story might sound, I usually go away from visiting her with a smile on my face. If she could read my story she'd laugh and say, "Mary, you're full of shit!"

9249* by Mary Haylock

Author Profile

Mary Haylock is a retired teacher with the Hamilton Board of Education, having spent 38 years working in the field of education. She graduated from McMaster University in Hamilton, Ontario in 1970 with a degree in English Literature. She recently (Nov. 2018) won an award for a short story she entered in a contest sponsored by the Hamilton Arts and Letters magazine.

Mary Haylock has also self published a book "A Nos/To Us" (ISBN-10:1452857792) under the pen name Ellen Homewood.

www.ingramcontent.com/pod-product-compliance
Lightning Source LLC
Chambersburg PA
CBHW072053110526
44590CB00018B/3157